Ghetto Kingdom

GHETTO KINGDOM

Tales of the Łódź Ghetto

ISAIAH SPIEGEL

Translated from the Yiddish by
David H. Hirsch & Roslyn Hirsch
and with an Introduction by David H. Hirsch

NORTHWESTERN UNIVERSITY PRESS
Evanston, Illinois

Northwestern University Press
Evanston, Illinois 60208-4210

Translation copyright © 1998 by Northwestern University Press. Introduction copyright © 1998 by Northwestern University Press. Published
1998. All rights reserved.

Printed in the United States of America

ISBN 0-8101-1624-3 (cloth)
ISBN 0-8101-1625-1 (paper)

Library of Congress Cataloging-in-Publication Data

Spiegel, Isaiah, 1906–
    [Short stories. English. Selections]
    Ghetto kingdom : tales of the Łódź ghetto / Isaiah Spiegel ;
translated from the Yiddish by David H. Hirsch & Roslyn Hirsch.
        p. cm. — (Jewish lives)
    Includes bibliographical references.
    ISBN 0-8101-1624-3 (cloth : alk. paper). — ISBN 0-8101-1625-1
(pbk. : alk. paper)
    1. Holocaust, Jewish (1939–1945)—Poland—Łódź—Fiction. 2.
Jews—Poland—Łódź—Fiction. 3. Spiegel, Isaiah, 1906–
—Translations into English. I. Hirsch, David H. II. Hirsch, Roslyn.
III. Title. IV. Series.
PJ5129.S6812A27 1998
839'.134—dc21   98-35270
                                                                CIP

❖

Contents

❁

Introduction to the
Ghetto Stories of Isaiah Spiegel

David H. Hirsch

Having survived nearly five years in the Łódź Ghetto, Auschwitz, and several labor camps, Isaiah Spiegel experienced in his own life the pathos that permeates the lives of the characters he portrayed in the short stories he wrote in the Łódź Ghetto during the years 1940–44.

Born into poverty in Baluty (Balut in Yiddish), a poor suburb of the Polish industrial city of Łódź, and eventually the site of the Łódź Ghetto, Spiegel received a Jewish upbringing, though he says his father was "not a pious Jew, he was a cultural Jew [*folks-yid*]."¹ Spiegel's father worked as a laborer in the weaving trade, and Spiegel's parents, though poor, lived what he described as "a disciplined life of quiet dignity."² He wrote, in an autobiographical preface to his book *Light from the Abyss* (CYCO, 1952), "My father and mother truly came from the folk. They were members of the exploited working masses, and lived unobtrusive upright lives. Though we often went hungry, the benevolence and unselfishness of my parents nurtured the years of my childhood, and blessed them with the inextinguishable charisma and grace of the Yiddish folk-soul."³ Spiegel attended a cheder (one-room school where Jewish subjects were taught) and a Talmud Torah, for more advanced Jewish studies. He continued to pursue his education in a normal school and then a teachers' seminary. At the outbreak of war in 1939, Spiegel, then thirty-three years old, was a teacher of Yiddish language and literature.

Subsequently, Spiegel survived the Łódź Ghetto, Auschwitz, and several other Nazi camps, but his parents and three of his sisters were murdered in the death camps. His wife was murdered in the death camp of Stutthof, and his only daughter died of starvation while still in the Łódź Ghetto. Spiegel returned to Łódź after the war, where he resumed teaching school till 1948. From 1948 to 1950, he lived in Warsaw, and in 1951, he emigrated to Israel, where he worked as a government clerk until 1964, when he was granted early retirement, owing to illness. In Israel, he continued to write stories, poems, novels, and essays in Yiddish.

All the stories included in the present collection are about the Łódź Ghetto, and most of them were actually written there, though they were revised later. Presided over by the highly controversial Chaim Rumkowski ("King of the Jews," as he was sometimes called), the Łódź Ghetto was the first of the Jewish ghettos to be created in German-occupied Poland (May 1940) and the last to be liquidated (August 1944).[4] Despite the physical and psychological deprivations and miseries Spiegel had to endure as an inmate of the Łódź Ghetto, he managed to keep writing, though the very act of writing exposed him to danger. In her memoir, Lucille Eichengreen, who was a trusted friend of Speigel's during the ghetto years, and who remained his devoted friend till the end of his life, remembers Spiegel's dismay when he learned that she was planning to take a position working directly for Rumkowski.

> Szaja looked at me aghast. "You'd be playing with fire. Rumkowski is a pig. I don't even consider him a human being. Two years ago, before you arrived in the ghetto, I wrote a song about a small infant in a crib, the father scrounging for food to feed his family and not succeeding. Rumkowski heard about it and thought it was an insult. He threatened me and created a ruling that outlawed my writing. It was only with the intervention of Henryk Neftalin that he agreed to leave me alone. I in turn promised to ignore him in my poetry and prose."[5]

Spiegel almost kept that promise. The only direct allusion to Rumkowski in the ghetto stories we know of is the following: "all the fields of innumerable raspberries were the property of one Jew—The Eldest of the Jews of the Litzmannstadt Ghetto" (See "Enchanted Fruit").[6]

Spiegel's writings did not go entirely unnoticed, and his talent did not go unrecognized by Yiddish literati. In addition to his novels and collections of short stories, his essays, poems, and fiction were published in Yiddish periodicals, both in Israel and the United States (*Die Goldene Keit* [The golden chain] and *Tzukunft* [The future], among others), and he was awarded several literary prizes.[7] But Spiegel wrote in Yiddish at a time when the use of Yiddish was being officially discouraged, and even disparaged, in Israel, and he was writing stories about Jews as victims at a time when the main thrust of Israeli ideology was to downplay a two-thousand-year history of Jewish passivity and persecution. Moreover, Spiegel, like other Yiddish writers, was cut off from a large audience because after the Holocaust there was no longer a Yiddish reading public that could support Yiddish writers; his natural audience had been decimated by the Nazis. Isaiah Spiegel died in Israel in 1991.

In Y. L. Peretz's classic story, "Bontsha the Silent," the narrator says of the title character, "In loneliness he lived, and in loneliness he died." While it would be an exaggeration to say the same of Spiegel, it is nevertheless the case that he never was accorded the recognition and acclaim he deserved.

The year after Spiegel's *Ghetto Kingdom* was published in Łódź, Poland (1947), there appeared in New York a brilliant study of the Yiddish writer, Y. L. Peretz. Maurice Samuel's *Prince of the Ghetto* was a glowing tribute to the greatest of Yiddish writers, and also a requiem of sorts to the Yiddish language and Yiddish literature. Samuel had visited Warsaw in 1919, and though by that time Peretz had been dead for four years, the Jews Samuel met in Warsaw spoke of Peretz as though he were still alive; Peretz, as Samuel puts it, "was one of those national phenomena which are unintelligible apart from their people's history. . . . His conscious task was the intellectual improvement of his people. He was obsessed by the spiritual and physical destiny of Jewry as Mazzini was by the spiritual and physical destiny of Italy."[8] Samuel adds about his visit to Poland: "Chiefly I recall from that time in Poland an extraordinary Jewish aliveness and a fantastic blossoming of hope—the spirit of Yal Peretz. They and he—the three and a quarter million Jews of Poland and Yal

Peretz—believed that a better time was coming!"⁹ Writing in
1948, Samuel was fully conscious of the irony of history, and of
how unwarranted that Jewish spirit of optimism in 1919 turned
out to be. In about a five-year period—from September 1939 to
June 1945—some three million of the "three and a quarter million" Polish Jews had been wiped out, and the nearly thousand-
year presence of Yiddish culture in Eastern Europe, and specifi-
cally in Poland, had been effectively terminated.

Spiegel, like all Yiddish writers of his generation, was heir to a
tradition enriched by his immediate predecessors. But while
Peretz could still conceive of working for "the spiritual and physical destiny of Jewry" in a free Poland, it became Spiegel's fate to
portray, in his fiction, the extermination of the Jewish community in Poland, and to record the struggle of Polish Jewry to preserve its spiritual integrity, even as it was being annihilated.

While the characters in Spiegel's stories often find themselves
paralyzed by the Nazi onslaught, Spiegel himself retained the will
and the ability to convert the hell of ghetto life into literary works
of art. Under the harshest living conditions imaginable (which he
describes so graphically in his fiction), Spiegel wrote short stories. Unlike the many diarists and chroniclers of ghetto life,
Spiegel did not become a writer solely in response to his ghetto
experience. He was a poet and a storyteller who had started pub-
lishing poetry in the early twenties.

Though he started writing poems at the height of the mod-
ernist movement, Spiegel was not very much influenced, either in
his poetry or prose, by literary modernism, or by the wave of
experimentalism that characterized European fiction in the first
decades of the twentieth century. In the introduction to their
anthology of Yiddish short stories, Howe and Greenberg have
noted that "Yiddish literature, particularly the prose, is poor in
formal experimentation."¹⁰ For Yiddish writers, they observe,
"Literature had to be *justified*, it had to be assigned a moral sanc-
tion. . . . For whatever its limitations of scope and form, Yiddish
literature is endowed with a moral poise, a security of values that
is very rare in any age."¹¹

Spiegel is heir to this tradition of morally engaged storytellers who portray the lives of simple people oppressed by both fate and society. "To this day," he has remarked, "I hear and understand the speech of poor people. Something of the mysterious essence of that world of the poor has crept into my very soul."[12] As did his predecessors, Spiegel treats his characters with compassion, but does not idealize them. It is hard to say what kind of stories Spiegel might have written had he not been sucked into the Nazi maelstrom, but indications are that he would have documented the hard lives of working-class Jews in Poland. The groundwork for writing about, and even celebrating, the humble folk had been established by the three founders, and giants, of Yiddish literature, Mendele Moykher Sforim, Sholem Aleichem, and Peretz.[13] The literary tradition they established has been described as "a literature that explored poverty as few others have, that studied the misery of this life . . . intensely."[14]

When asked by Yechiel Szeintuch, "How are you, personally, indebted to Mendele, Sholem Aleichem, and Peretz?" Spiegel replied that although he had been influenced by all three, he felt closest to Mendele: "To be perfectly truthful," he said, "I had the greatest affection for Mendele. . . . All I have to do is just touch one of his books to realize how much of him I carry within me— his rare essence, his language, his laughter, his wisdom, his succinct style, his strong ties to the Jewish community, and his hidden tear, evoked by the social oppression in which his characters lived. And yet it is that tear that lights up Mendele's world and is his great talent, and that is what I love in him."[15]

Not surprisingly, Spiegel's long-suffering Jews are not very different from those his predecessors wrote about in their fiction. But the living conditions Spiegel's characters had to endure under Nazi rule had deteriorated precipitously from the unrelieved poverty of the shtetl to the genocide being committed in the ghetto. The level of human misery from shtetl to ghetto had been ratcheted up several notches in a very short time. The hunger, suffering, cruelty, and breakdown of community that took place in the Łódź ghetto went infinitely beyond the miseries of the "ordinary" poverty and oppression suffered by Jews living in the shtetls and urban slums of Eastern Europe, and beyond what any writer could have anticipated in the nineteenth and early twenti-

eth centuries. Whereas earlier Yiddish writers had portrayed the
hand-to-mouth existence of Jews living in poverty, Spiegel inher-
ited the task of describing people being deliberately starved to
death, being murdered both systematically and at random. While
the impoverished Jews of the shtetl had found a way of retaining
their human dignity by setting up humane social and cultural
institutions, and cultivating faith in a consoling and redemptive
God, the Nazi onslaught was designed to obliterate human dignity and destroy any possibility of believing in a just and caring
God.

The characters in Spiegel's story, "The Death of Anna Nikolayevna Temkin" (dated 1941 by Szeintuch), might well have
come right out of one of the stories of his predecessors, especially his beloved Mendele. The tale is framed by a more or less
chummy first-person naive narrator who is, in a sense, part of the
story, and who describes himself as coming from the working
classes:

> Unfortunately, I can't tell you much about the origins of Anna
> Nikolayevna Temkin, because I myself, you should know, don't
> come from the gentry. On the contrary, my family origins are
> quite humble. We are plain folk. . . . My father . . . didn't wander
> far from his father's humble trade. He was a weaver in his youth
> and afterwards supported me, the eldest, and the rest of the chil-
> dren, by manufacturing little cardboard wallets that he sold to
> storekeepers.[16]

The title character, Anna, is a befuddled and inoffensive Jewish
woman who, before the war, had lived a comfortable existence. In
the ghetto, however, the tables are turned. There, the poor Jews
who have always lived on the margin have had an easier time
adjusting to the new ghetto reality than Anna, who has had to
learn to live without her customary support systems and without
her bodily comforts. Although Howe and Greenberg minimize
the importance of class conflict in Yiddish culture and literature,
it seems that Spiegel, in this early story, intended to use class conflict for comic purposes. When Anna, who mixes Russian words
into her "Lithuanian" Yiddish (which was considered more cul-

tured and literary than other dialects of Yiddish), asks someone for directions, the person she has addressed bitterly mimics her and denounces what he takes to be her affectations:

> "Izvinitye Gospodin, do me a favor, uncle [she used to speak Russian and then immediately translate into Lithuanian Yiddish], where is Krutke Alley?"
>
> "Well, take a look at the fine lady who honors us with her presence!" was the angry answer she got from a man with an empty pot in his hand. "I'm glad to see you find our neighborhood so much to your liking now. When did such a grand lady ever come here before? Did she ever come to see how her own brothers and sisters were living? Huh? Never. You could have gone a whole lifetime. But now! To hell with the whole pack of them. They always lived high on the hog up there in their swell places, and you could never get anywhere near them. The high fancy doors were always locked, and in front of the gate was the goy [gentile], may he be cursed. But now? A hearty welcome to you! Izvinitye Gospodin," he says, mimicking Anna Nikolayevna's voice, "Gdye is Krutke Alley? Blast them all to damn hell!"

Written in 1941, this story antedates the most oppressive phase of existence in the Łódź Ghetto, and though Spiegel never quite fully lost his sense of humor and his consciousness of class distinctions among Jews, the stories become more somber and despairing as the situation of the Jews in the ghetto becomes more desperate. In the last stages of the extermination process, distinctions among victims tended to disappear. The closing paragraph of the story suggests that Spiegel, at this stage of ghetto existence, was thinking of a short-story cycle told by a narrator who would act, to paraphrase Joyce, as "the uncreated conscience of his race."

At first glance, Spiegel's stories seem to be direct representations of ghetto reality, but no one would think so who has read some of the many journals and diaries kept in the ghetto. There were, in fact, brilliant diarists in many of the ghettos. Probably none of these diaries is better known (and deservedly so) than

Chaim Kaplan's *Diary of the Warsaw Ghetto* (originally given the English title, *Scroll of Agony*). Kaplan was a thinker and an intellectual. For purposes of security, he wrote in Hebrew, and the diary was intended to bear witness to the destruction taking place around him. Kaplan was fluent in Polish, German, Russian, and Yiddish, as well as Hebrew, and his diary is more than descriptive. Kaplan not only depicts, with amazing foresight, the terrible events unfolding before him, but speculates on the future prospects of humanity, and shows great insights into human behavior. One need go no further than the first entry in the English version, September 1, 1939, the day of the German invasion. Kaplan recorded, with notable prescience: "This war will indeed bring destruction upon human civilization. But this is a civilization which merits annihilation and destruction. There is no doubt that Hitlerian Nazism will ultimately be defeated, for in the end the civilized nations will rise up to defend the liberty which the German barbarians seek to steal from mankind. However, I doubt that we will live through this carnage."[17]

Kaplan's foresight is uncanny, and his analyses of the political and military situation are brilliant. Though Kaplan did not intend the diary as a self-advertisement, it bears stunning witness to the anguished and tortured soul that created it; the diary reveals a mature and highly learned mind, an extraordinary human being of impeccable moral integrity. Written as a journey into the human soul, Kaplan's diary, with its enlightened Euro-Judaic humanism, represents the very antithesis of Nazi barbarism.[18]

Spiegel was more of an autodidact than Kaplan, but he is the only writer we know of who was able to write an extended collection of short stories inside the ghetto.[19] Even if the fiction sometimes seems to be no more than a thinly disguised record of actual events, it is still fiction. Unlike the ghetto diarists, Spiegel was moved to convert the ghetto horrors not only into language but into works of art. Many of the stories in this collection are surely worthy of that designation, "works of art."[20] Though lyrical passages abound in Spiegel's stories, their artfulness does not consist in painting pretty pictures or in creating objects of evanescent beauty, but rather in embodying truth in symbolic structures. Artworks of this kind are not as unusual as some commentators on Holocaust literature would have us believe. The great Yiddish writers, as well as other fiction writers of the late nineteenth and early twentieth centuries in Europe and America, conceived literature primarily as the art of casting bitter truths into narrative forms; they were members of the naturalist and/or realist school. The American naturalist Stephen Crane wrote a novella about "The girl Maggie, [who] blossomed in a mud puddle." In the story, Crane described, with both outrage and a strong sense of compassion, the moral degradation of slum life, without romanticizing the slum dwellers.

Spiegel's stories, as symbolic structures, convey the ghetto horror without being overwhelmed by the unprecedented cruelties of ghetto life. In an early and highly perceptive review, Sh[muel] Niger pointed out that while Spiegel

> always feels the stinging pain of truth and conscience, he is even more sensitive to dreams, and since no person living in a state of constant distress and in a reality of unabated horror gives up the world of dreams willingly, Spiegel's *Ghetto Kingdom* is a kingdom of dreams. True enough, it is a hapless kingdom pervaded by death, but it is a realm, nonetheless, immersed in dreams.

Niger goes on to say that the "unexpected transformations" we find in Spiegel's stories "constitute the secret, the magic, of Spiegel's ghetto kingdom. Out of the dark truth of the ghetto emerges a tearfully luminous dream. . . . Does that mean [Spiegel's fiction] is idealized, or romantic? No, the stories are completely realistic."[21]

Chaim Kaplan, as he comes to life in his diary entries, becomes a living refutation of Nazi ideology. It is as if Kaplan knew that he had to keep asserting both his humanity and his belief in an enlightened biblical-rabbinical humanism in the face of the antihuman Nazi assault, even though it was possible that the diary itself would never see the light of day. But there are no Chaim Kaplans in the ghetto stories written by Spiegel: only simple people with more than their share of human weakness—vulgar, coarse, greedy, vulnerable, self-centered human beings who have been pushed to unprecedented extremes. In the ultimate extreme, survival becomes the supreme value for most people.

Where Spiegel as a short-story writer diverges from the diarists, no matter how noble and talented some of them may have been, is in his creation of a fictional world (let us say like Sherwood Anderson's Winesburg, or Faulkner's Yoknapatawpha County). Though the world of Spiegel's stories may be a reflection, or representation, of the Łódź Ghetto, it is also a world that takes on its own existence in the stories. Above all else, the ghetto world was an antiworld, a world ruled by Satan rather than God, as conveyed succinctly in the lyrics of the concentration camp song "Birkenau":

> Birkenau, cierniowa droga,
> Milionów ofiar wspólny grób.
> Królewstwo zła, gdzie niema boga.
> To Birkenau.

> (Birkenau, thorny path,
> Where millions of victims lie in a common grave.
> Evil kingdom, where there is no God.
> This is Birkenau.)[22]

Speigel's stories, because they are fiction, can re-create this antiworld in a way that journals and diaries do not. The philosopher Emmanuel Levinas says, in one of his well-known essays, "I have just read a text which is both beautiful and real—as real as only fiction can be."[23] The same may be said of Spiegel's stories.

In part, Spiegel creates the antiworld of the ghetto with an adjectival style, as may be perceived in the opening paragraph of the title story of the collection, *Ghetto Kingdom:*

> A pale streak of amorphous light ripped the night sky hung with heavy clouds resembling tattered worn black garments. It looked as though the retiring night demons had lashed the face of the diffuse night clouds with a birch whip, staining the entire length of

the eastern horizon with a reddish-brown streak, like congealed blood on the face of a smitten human being. The surrounding clouds, dark and swollen, stepped to the side and floated away shamefacedly, as the infinitely extended stripe exploded into bright spots of color, innumerable red tassels, and strands of thread. A predawn wind from out of nowhere that had somehow blundered into the ghetto with the gray morning light suddenly assaulted the clouds, which dissipated into countless fragments of color. Then the sky suddenly turned a transparent white. In the east, poised on the edge of day and night, the earth seemed to split, and out of the chasm rose the flattened head of sad red sun that gave off no rays. That ruddy head remained suspended on the rooftops, and peered out from above them without moving from the spot. Elsewhere in the sky, the remaining strips of clouds grew thinner and finally melted away completely.[24]

This is one of Spiegel's great stories, and in it he captures the essential distinction between the normal world and the ghetto world. The ghetto world is a nightmare world. In the ghetto, nightmare is reality. In this opening description, the sky that enters the ghetto is not the same sky that covers the rest of the world. The clouds in the ghetto are not the same clouds that float in other skies. They have taken on the ghetto countenance and thus resemble "tattered worn black garments." The sun is not the same sun. Everything in the ghetto is distorted, disfigured, situated at a peculiar angle. Gray is the dominant color of the ghetto world. Even the sun does not send out its rays as it does in the normal world. A little further on in the text, the grays and rotting greens are set in contrast to the "gold Star of David patches" and to the redness of blood. With masterful artistic symmetry, the image of the reddish-brown streak of the opening paragraph returns in the last paragraph, where "the Crucified One in the heart of the ghetto is now drenched in flame. His thin tortured Jewish body lies curled in a red pool of warm blood."

In the English introduction to the manuscript stories, Szeintuch asserts that "Spiegel's famous story *Malches Geto* [Ghetto kingdom] does not refer to 'King' Rumkowski, but to 'King'

Hunger."[25] The beauty of fictional images, however, is that they are suggestive and convey shades of meaning. Hence, the ghetto kingdom is Rumkowski's kingdom and also a kingdom of hunger. But the ghetto kingdom is also a parody of the kingdom of God and a bitter commentary on Rumkowski's delusion that he was a messiah who, by delivering as many Jews as necessary to Moloch, would eventually turn out to be a savior of a remnant of the Jews.[26]

Unlike most of Spiegel's ghetto tales, which focus on the lives of individual characters, "Ghetto Kingdom" presents a portrait of life in general during a single day in the ghetto, including the pervasive, desperate hunger, the ubiquitous terror, and the unrelieved suffering. The story, though short, is divided into three scenes. The first is a scene of early morning, where the mouselike ghetto dwellers come pouring out of their meager hovels to begin the endless and all too often futile search for food. The second scene portrays a market that seems to appear out of nowhere, which then modulates into a dreamlike market of the past. And finally, the scene shifts to evening and the Holy Mary Church, which has been enclosed in the ghetto. The church, which actually was left behind in the historically existent Łódź Ghetto, introduces a rich strain of Christian imagery that serves to link the suffering of the present-day Jews to the present-day Christians who have abandoned their Christian values and no longer seem to live in accord with their Christian beliefs or in conformity to their Christian consciences.

The image of the church, which the Poles were forced to abandon, suggests an abandonment of not only the building, but of the moral beliefs that once were presumably promulgated there. Like the Jews themselves, the church is "fenced in, trapped inside the Jewish ghetto." As a consequence of Chaim Rumkowski's policy of trying to save a remnant of Jews by making the ghetto productive for the Germans, the church has been turned into a bedding factory. But it is not an ordinary bedding factory; rather, it is one in which stolen "down and feathers, stained with blood and dampened with Jewish tears, have been brought from the surrounding hamlets" to be reworked. In keeping with Nazi ideology, which both Jews and Poles are powerless to change, the holy site, like the people, has been turned into not only an industrial enterprise, but a criminal enterprise.[27]

And yet, the holy place retains some of its supernatural nuances: "Various holy saints are standing on the sills of the narrow windows, looking down with tearful gilded eyes at the Jews running about below. A golden light seems to descend from their round faces and the sunny halos around their heads, as a zephyr stirs among the bells." Stripped of their own sacred symbols and texts, deprived of their own gathering places to worship in, the Jews find themselves enveloped in the mysterious sonorities of the abandoned church, and what emerges is a strange union between the present-day ghetto Jews and the biblical origins of Christianity. The symbols of Christianity have come to be far more closely tied to the imprisoned Jews than to the Christians outside the ghetto, who have abandoned the moral principles those symbols stand for, and it is now the Jews gathered in the church who pray in a mixture of Yiddish and Hebrew: "Master of the Universe, be merciful to your people, Israel. . . . Have pity on your wretched people!"

The final paragraph seals the connection between the Jews enclosed in the ghetto and the historical Israelite origins of Christianity by focusing on the most powerful image of the Christian faith, the image of the crucified Jesus:

> On a side street not far from the church is a small brick chapel with an "eternal light" burning inside, and above the light a plaster statue of the Crucified One. The darker it gets outside, the more vivid glows the red light beneath the Crucified One. Once again the wind whistles around the tower clock. Night has already fallen on the windows of the Ghetto Kingdom. The holy flame from the little chapel lashes the face of the last Jew as he runs through the narrow street. Boots are pounding on the other side of the wire. Germans are entering the ghetto. The Crucified One in the heart of the ghetto is now drenched in flame. His thin tortured Jewish body lies curled in a red pool of warm blood.

The final sentence establishes a link between "the last Jew" hurrying home to beat the curfew and the crucified Jesus. Both are emaciated and tortured. Here, the full ironic significance of the presence of the symbols of Christianity in the ghetto is underscored. Certain strains of Christian theology had long labeled the Jews as Christ killers. Spiegel's imagery reminds the reader that the gentiles, by persecuting the Jews and abandoning them to the killers, contribute to the reenactment of the crucifixion many times each day.

By stressing the link between Christ and the Jews in the ghetto, Spiegel is able to set the persecution of the Jews into a wider historical perspective. Spiegel's use of the image of the crucifixion in the deserted chapel allows him to focus on the Christians' blatant violation of Christian morality. With the sentence, "Night has already fallen on the windows of the Ghetto Kingdom," we are reminded that at the crucifixion, as reported in the Gospels, the "accusation" or "superscription" is set above Jesus's head: "This is Jesus the King of the Jews" (Matt. 27:37; also, Mark 15:26; Luke 23:37–38; John 19:19–22). Even if the name of Chaim Rumkowski is not mentioned, it is difficult to overlook the parodic connection between Jesus, King of the Jews, and King Chaim, who believed he was the Messiah.[28] A biblical commentator has remarked that the "titulus was plainly a warning to the Jews. It said in letters of blood as well as of gypsum, 'This is what will happen to you if you try to defy the empire.'"[29] There are several ironies here, foremost, of course, being the parallel between the self-anointed messiah, Rumkowski, and the crucified Jew, Jesus (whom many of those killing Jews believed to be the true Messiah). One is also reminded that in Luke's version, a mocker cries out, "If thou be the king of the Jews, save thyself" (23:37). As Jesus cannot save himself, neither can Rumkowski save himself or the Jews.

Spiegel plays a variation on the motif of the false messiah in the brilliant story "The Sampolne Rebbe," where two religious sects in the ghetto use arcane methods of interpreting mystical texts to discover the meaning of the events overtaking the ghettoized Jews. One sect interprets the signs as a forecast of the dissolution of the world, while the other interprets the upheavals as a manifestation of *chevlei moishiach*, the "birth pangs of the Messiah," a time of troubles and turbulence that precedes the coming of the

Messiah. In this allegorical tale, Spiegel satirizes the longing of Jews for the coming of the Messiah,[30] and, at the same time, he ridicules the faith of the ghetto dwellers in the false messiah, Rumkowski. There are many more treasures in this collection, including such stories as "Bread," "The Workbench," "The Singing of the Birds," "Blossoms," and others. Also precious is Spiegel's depiction of the absurd, but all too human, conflict between the "*Ostjuden*" (Eastern Jews) and German Jews, a conflict that arises when the Nazis start deporting Jews from Western Europe to the Łódź Ghetto. In the stories, "Jews" and "The Sorcerer," Spiegel handles the clash of two Jewish cultures in a time of crisis with humor and compassion.[31] But it is beyond the scope of this introduction to discuss all these marvelous stories in detail.

It may be appropriate to bring this introduction to a close by giving the last word to another Yiddish writer eminently qualified to assess Spiegel's artistic achievement. Reviewing the short-story collection, *Mentshn in tehom* (People in the Abyss) (Buenos Aires, 1949), Jacob Glatstein, a poet, essayist, and man of letters, rendered homage to Spiegel as a literary craftsman and as the creator of a profoundly moving fictional world:

> Writers sometimes experience a rare emotion that may be even stronger than the envy they often feel toward fellow writers. . . . At such times, the writer experiences an intensified humility. He feels a renewed sense of wonder in the presence of the written word. . . . That rare feeling . . . is . . . the love felt for another's labor, a love that possesses the writer-reader so completely that he feels the deepest gratitude toward the other author and his work. The reader loses all consciousness of being in the presence of an artifact, and becomes so completely involved in the work that he is elevated into a realm of being in which he can no longer distinguish between art and life. . . . When I read Isaiah Spiegel's ghetto stories in his new book—I felt that shock of recognition . . . , that love of the author you feel reading the work of writers like Sholem Aleichem, Mendele, Peretz, and H. N. Bialik.[32]

Notes

1. Isaiah Spiegel, interview by Yechiel Szeintuch, in Yechiel Szeintuch and Vera Solomon, eds., *Isaiah Spiegel—Yiddish Narrative Prose from the Łódź Ghetto* (Jerusalem: The Magnes Press, 1995), p. 249; hereafter cited as *Yiddish Narrative Prose*.

2. Ibid.

3. Quoted in Charlotte Spiegel, "Biographical and Bibliographical Data," (Yiddish) in *Licht in Tehom* (Light in the abyss) (Tel Aviv: Israel Book, 1976), 2: 281.

4. For a detailed account of the history of the Łódź Ghetto, see the introduction to *The Chronicle of the Łódź Ghetto: 1941-1944*, ed. Lucjan Dobroszycki, trans. Richard Lourie et al. (New Haven, Conn.: Yale University Press, 1984), pp. ix–lxvii; hereafter cited as *The Chronicle*.

5. Lucille Eichengreen, with Harriet Hyman Chamberlain, *From Ashes to Life: My Memories of the Holocaust* (San Francisco: Mercury House, 1994), p. 72.

6. The title of the original is *"A Yid fun beis oilam"* (A Jew from the cemetery). Litzmannstadt was the name given to Łódź by the Germans.

7. He was awarded a number of literary prizes in Israel, France, and the United States, and was celebrated with a jubilee in 1966, and a jubilee volume, *In Licht fun der Farloshener Pen* (In the light of the extinguished pen) (Tel Aviv: Israel Book, 1986); hereafter cited as *Extinguished Pen*.

8. Maurice Samuel, *Prince of the Ghetto* (New York: Knopf, 1948), pp. 5–6.

9. Ibid., p. 8.

10. Irving Howe and Eliezer Greenberg, *A Treasury of Yiddish Stories* (New York: Viking Press, 1954), p. 36.

11. Ibid., pp. 31, 37.

12. Spiegel, in *Yiddish Narrative Prose*, p. 248.

13. Mendele, née S. Y. Abramovitsh (1836–1917), is credited with being the founder of modern Yiddish literature; Sholem Aleichem, née Sholem Rabinovitsh (1859–1916), the great humorist, is best known to English readers for the Tevye tales, which were popularized as *Fiddler on the Roof*, and he has often

been compared to Mark Twain; Y. L. Peretz (1852-1915), a versatile man of letters and great short-story writer, is remembered for his classic story, "Bontshe the Silent," and for his retelling of chassidic tales. See Ken Frieden's excellent presentation of these writers in *Classic Yiddish Fiction* (Albany: SUNY Press, 1995). Like his predecessors, Spiegel read, and was influenced by, both Polish and Russian writers. Reading Spiegel's ghetto stories, one is often reminded of Gogols's grotesques, and in his interviews with Szeintuch, Spiegel describes at length his reading of the nineteenth-century Polish writer, Eliza Orzeszkowa. Compare, also, Yisrael Rabon's novel about impoverished Jews in Łódź, *D. Gas* (The street), brilliantly translated by Leonard Wolf (New York: Schocken, 1985).

14. Frieden, *Classic Yiddish Fiction,* p. 38.

15. Spiegel, *Yiddish Narrative Prose,* p. 280.

16. Spiegel, *Ghetto Kingdom,* pp. 17–18.

17. *Scroll of Agony: The Warsaw Diary of Chaim A. Kaplan,* rev. ed., trans. and ed. Abraham I. Katsh (New York: Macmillan, 1973), p. 19.

18. Writings left behind by Emmanuel Ringelblum and David Lewin are both touching and knowledgeable. *The Chronicle,* cited in n. 4, is a repository of factual information about the Łódź Ghetto.

19. There are some remarkable narratives, such as "Dawid Sierakowiak's Diary," selections from which appear in Alan Adelson and Robert Lapides, eds., *Łódź Ghetto: Inside a Community Under Siege* (New York: Penguin Books, 1989), pp. 7–18. Some very powerful poetry was written in both Yiddish and Polish in the Warsaw and Vilna Ghettos, among others.

20. Of course, one need not live among horrors to write about them, as witness Edgar Allan Poe, H. P. Lovecraft, and other writers of horror fiction.

21. Sh[muel] Niger, "Stars Over the Ghetto," in *Extinguished Pen,* p. 10.

22. Aleksander Kulisiewicz, from the recording *Piesni Obozowe* (Concentration camp songs) (Polskie Nagrania: Muza, SX1715).

23. Emmanuel Levinas, "To Love the Torah More Than God,"

Difficult Freedom (Baltimore: Johns Hopkins University Press, 1990), p. 142

24. This descriptive opening paragraph, different from the translation on p. 110, is not in the manuscript version of the story, which begins with the ghetto dwellers pouring out of their ghetto hovels.

25. Szeintuch, *Yiddish Narrative Prose,* p. xiii.

26. See Philip Friedman, "Pseudo-Saviors in the Polish Ghettos: Mordechai Chaim Rumkowski of Łódź," in *Roads to Extinction,* ed. Ada Friedman (Philadelphia: Jewish Publication Society, 1980), pp. 333–52. This essay also provides a very readable brief history of the Łódź Ghetto.

27. *The Chronicle,* following p. 424, contains a picture of the church alluded to, the Most Blessed Virgin Mary Church, showing the piles of confiscated down and feathers.

28. See Friedman, "Pseudo-Saviors," pp. 333–34, 336.

29. *The Interpreter's Bible,* 12 vols. (New York and Nashville: Abingdon Press, 1951), 7: 605.

30. See *Encyclopedia Judaica,* first printing, 1971, s.v. "Messianic Movements."

31. For a historical account of the deportation of German Jews to the Łódź Ghetto, see *The Chronicle,* pp. lvii–lix; 78 fn. 92, 80–81, passim.

32. The review appeared in *Der Yiddisher Kempfer* (The Jewish fighter) (July 28, 1950), and is reprinted in *Extinguished Pen,* pp. 37, 39.

❀

A Note on the Text

Before being deported to Auschwitz, Spiegel had managed to bury his manuscript stories in a cellar. After he was liberated, he retrieved many of the manuscripts he had left behind. He found sixteen, though there are rumors that more manuscripts were found subsequently and remain in private hands. The sixteen known manuscripts have been edited and published by Yechiel Szeintuch.[1]

Spiegel revised some of the retrieved manuscripts and apparently reconstructed (or perhaps wrote from scratch) additional stories immediately after his liberation; in 1947, the collection *Malchus Getto* (Ghetto kingdom) was published in Łódź. There were eleven stories in this collection, which are all included in the present collection. Manuscript versions exist for five of these stories.[2] In 1948, the collection *Shtern Ibern Getto* (Stars over the ghetto) was published in Paris. Four of the six stories in the 1948 collection are included in the present edition, and four are extant in manuscript versions.[3] Two stories in the present collection ("The Sampolne Rebbe" and "Enchanted Fruit") were translated from a two-volume collection, *Shtern Leichtn in Tehom* (Stars shine in the abyss) (Tel Aviv, 1976).

We tried to preserve the immediacy and authenticity of the stories by translating from the first published versions (1947, 1948), but we also consulted the revised versions, in keeping with the editorial principle of honoring the author's final intention. Where a later revision was more lucid, or clearly superior aesthetically, or made an important point, we used it. But we should make clear that there are not many differences between the first published stories and the revised versions, and most of the revisions are very minor indeed.

Changes from the manuscripts to the first published versions are sometimes (but not consistently) more significant; however, these are not a matter of primary concern for us, because we are presenting the stories as aesthetically worthy fictions that reflect the author's final intention. We should also add that we have arranged the stories roughly according to the dates Spiegel assigned them in 1948 and in later editions. The stories in *Ghetto Kingdom* (1947) were not dated, but those in *Stars Over the Ghetto* (1948) were.[4] All the stories in the 1976 collection are dated. In arranging the stories in the present collection, we have also taken into consideration the putative relationship between events described in the stories and the historical situations to which those events correspond. For example, "Earth" is the first story in *Ghetto Kingdom,* and the fictional events that occur in the story correspond to historical events that took place in September 1939, when Germany invaded Poland.

We have also included a translation of the manuscript story, "The Death of Anna Nikolayevna Temkin," which can stand on its own as a completed work of fiction. Edited by Yechiel Szeintuch and Vera Solomon, the story was first published in 1990, in the literary journal, *Die Goldene Keit* (The golden chain) (Tel Aviv) no. 130, and is reprinted in Szeintuch's edition of the manuscript stories.[5] "The Death of Anna . . . " seems to have been the basis for a story later published under the title "Nikki." Translated by Bernard Guilbert Guerney, the story was included in the Irving Howe and Eliezer Greenberg anthology, *A Treasury of Yiddish Stories* (1954) as "A Ghetto Dog."

We would like to dedicate this translation to the memory of Ethel Friedfeld, a true Woman of Valor.

Notes

1. Yechiel Szeintuch and Vera Solomon, eds., *Isaiah Spiegel— Yiddish Narrative Prose from the Łódź Ghetto* (Jerusalem: The Magnes Press, 1995).

2. "Light from the Abyss" (MS title, "The Last Two"); "Earth" (MS title, "The Jew, Yossi Ber, of Dolne Yary"); "Ghetto

Kingdom"; "Sabbath Candles" (MS title, "Itte Blesses the Candelabra"); "Bread" (MS title, "Through a Crack").

3. "In a Death Alley," (titled "Straw" in the MS version). Aside from the retitling, this is one case where the MS and revised versions are almost identical; "The Family Lifschitz Moves to the Ghetto" (MS title, "They Were Cooking Beets"; this story is not included in the present collection); "In the Dark" (MS title, "The Third Party"); "The Workbench" (MS title, "A Vanished Life").

4. That is to say, Spiegel may have dated the stories from memory, after the fact, having adopted the custom of dating them at least as early as 1948.

5. The name of the title character in the manuscript version is Anna Yakovlevna Temkin.

Ghetto Kingdom

❖

Earth

Late one evening an unearthly clatter could be heard on the road between Ashene and Topoluvke. Flanked by fertile Polish fields, the road is very wide at this point and the moonlit Varta usually flows through the silence like a shiny silk ribbon. But this particular evening, screeching peasant carts and rickety hay wagons were raising a racket in all the remote villages along the main road to the city.

Darkness had descended, and an early autumn mist was rising from the low grasses and bushes, when the western horizon suddenly seemed to burst into flame, illuminated by streaks of fire. Jolted out of their sleep the terrified peasants in the villages around the Varta hastily packed their household goods, roused their wives and children from sleep, and loaded them into the harnessed wagons. They led the cows out of their warm stalls and tethered them to the bulging wagons with rope and chains. Cows lowed in the darkness with an eerie longing as they sadly permitted themselves to be fettered.

Sagging peasant wagons streamed out of all the villages of the region. The doors of the huts had been left open. Terrified fowl, roused from slumber, broke the night silence with the flapping of their wings. Caged pigeons joined chickens and geese in mournful screeching. Whimpering dogs under the wagons sounded like whining humans. Since yesterday, peasant vehicles from the villages nearest the front had been pouring toward the main highway. Shepherds prodded livestock whose hooves raised clouds of dust. Groups of peasants shuffled alongside the wagons, some with harmonicas dangling from their shoulders and some dragging dogs on thin leashes. Meanwhile, the reddish sky, spotted with clouds, stretched toward the multitudes like an unpaved road.

As the first group of peasants and wagons reached the edge of the forest where the highway forks to Dolny-Yary, Dobbe was feeding her two dogs, before going to bed. It was the same routine she had followed since childhood. Her husband, Yossi Ber, was already snoring under the thick comforter after a day's labor in the fields and the stable. The windows were half open, and the moist late September air, heavy with the aroma of forest branches set aside for winter, floated into the room.

In the darkness, the two dogs curled themselves at Dobbe's bare feet and stuck out their pointy muzzles. Suddenly both dogs leapt to their feet and began barking wildly. Dobbe had not heard anything unusual, but both dogs had detected the clattering of the first peasant wagons approaching Dolny-Yary. Dobbe ran out of the little yard and planted herself in the middle of the road, her bare feet wet from the grass and fallen leaves.

As the uproar came closer, it was possible to pick up the groan of the wagons and the sounds of human voices. The village of Dolny-Yary was still asleep as the first peasant wagons in the column rolled into the village. The advancing mob banged on the windows of every one of the low-roofed huts. In the early autumn darkness the alarm echoed from window to window, door to door!

"*Ida, ida! Ida! Niemcy ida!*" (They're coming, they're coming! They're coming! The Germans are coming!)

That ominous cry clanged like the tolling of a loud bell, waking up the village folk. Dobbe stood outside the hut drenched in a cold sweat. Seeing her shadowy figure, the first peasants to pass by told her the news. Dobbe, the thick peasant Jewess, felt as if her heart had just stopped beating. Everybody knew that war had broken out, but how was it possible that the Germans should have arrived here so quickly? Her head was in a whirl. She chased after one of the wagons in the darkness:

"*A dokad-to? Idzieci dokad to?*" (Where to? Where are you headed?) In her terror, she chased after the crowd, hoping for some scrap of good news.

"*Do Warszawy! Do Warszawy! Do Warszawy!*" (To Warsaw! To Warsaw! To Warsaw!) answered the terrified voices of the peasants, as they urged on their exhausted frightened animals.

Dobbe stood in the middle of the road as the mob slithered into the night like a gigantic black snake. The sky reddened with distant fires from the other side of the Varta. The lowing of the cows eventually modulated into an eerie sobbing. The last of the wagons heading toward the Warsaw highway passed through Dolny-Yary.

Dobbe kept standing there, in a trance. The dogs warmed her ankles with their fur. She stared into the dark village. Lighted lamps started appearing in the windows. Soon, a clamor arose from the cottages of Dolny-Yary, a banging of doors and windows, a screeching of wheels, and the rattle of wagons being pulled out of the stables by the awakened peasants. All their belongings were soon laid out in front of the door, alongside their sleeping children. Fettered cows were ready to take to the road.

Dobbe sat down next to a gully. The dogs laid their heads in her lap and remained silent.

Run away? Escape to Warsaw? A sliver of a thought popped into her mind. Where to? To whom? Where could she run?

Yossi Ber's Jewish ancestors had lived in the village for generations. After the death of his father, who had leased a piece of land and had acquired the peasant's knack for managing a farm, Yossi Ber was left with a substantial stable, a horse, a spotted cow, two goats, some chickens, and the two dogs. During the long years of farm work, the Jew grew to love the damp earth near the Varta river, the muted noise of the domestic animals and chickens, and the sunrise and sunset over the poplars of Dolny-Yary. Like his father and the rest of his family, Yossi Ber permitted the days of his life to float away in the cool waters of the Varta, living a quiet isolated existence alienated from Jewishness, a life confined to village walls and peasant labor. He sometimes felt a longing to socialize with a fellow Jew. At such times, mainly holidays or days of remembrance, he would pay a quick visit to a nearby Jewish shtetl where he could find a quorum, enabling him to recite the prayer for the dead in honor of his parents. He would then return at peace with himself and would once again devote himself to his work in the stable and on his piece of land.

At first the Polish peasants used to taunt him, but after a while the Jew's life melted into theirs, especially on Saturdays and Sundays; through the years, he attended weddings and funerals that took place in the town of Dolny-Yary near the flowing waters of the Varta.

Yossi Ber and his wife, Dobbe, had no children. They would start their day at the crack of dawn, as soon as the golden rays of the sun had sliced into the cool waters of the Varta. They gathered the fallen leaves, led the cows out to pasture, let out the chickens, then sat down on the threshold of the open doorway and looked down the sloping path that twisted its way to the flowing waters.

Whenever Yossi Ber and Dobbe considered leaving the village, so they could live among city people, including Jews, and not sink into complete boorishness here in the village among the peasants—at those moments Yossi Ber would be reminded of his father, Godel, with his thick fleshy nose and thick dark eyebrows, dressed in the cotton coat he wore all year round. His father would bend over him and ask: "Yossi Ber, Yossi Ber, where on earth do you think you're going? Where can you go? Your father lived here, your grandfather lived here, and they were Jews like all Jews. . . . You have no one to recite the prayer for the dead on your behalf. Stay on the land. Love the earth, and the earth will love you."

Finally, the couple stopped thinking of moving to the city. In the cool of morning Yossi Ber would sit on the banks of the Varta, catching fish to sell to Jews for the Sabbath. Twice a week he would ride to the shtetl with two cans of milk and a little butter and some eggs. Yossi Ber grew to love the moist earth, the cool gray water, the sound of the leaves on the slender poplars of Dolny-Yary. And, indeed, the earth and the water and the poplars came to love him too.

Dobbe was still sitting near the gully, the dogs at her side. The darkness had grown denser, even as the scarlet glow on the western horizon had grown brighter. The peasants of Dolny-Yary and their loaded wagons kept moving past her. The village had emptied out, except for some abandoned pigs who could be heard oinking behind fences hidden in darkness.

When Dobbe returned to the hut she found Yossi Ber standing in the middle of the room. The kerosene lamp on the bureau was filling the room with smoke. Yossi Ber knew everything. He had watched the hordes streaming past the window. He had seen the Polish patriots abandoning their ancestral homes to flee deeper into the homeland. Now Yossi Ber stood there forlorn, the glow of the lamp shimmering on his beard. He was barefoot and bareheaded. His wide nose was white with tension. The poplars in front of the little window could be heard swaying in the wind. Dobbe's hands started trembling.

"Yossi Ber," she called, not lifting her eyes from the floor, "the village is empty . . . not a living soul . . . just one Jew . . . let's save ourselves."

Yossi Ber lifted his head and looked into Dobbe's eyes. He said nothing. He just lowered his hands till they touched the two dogs, then he petted them on the muzzle.

"God be with you, Yossi Ber," his wife shouted. "Why don't you say something? For God's sake! God forbid, the Germans will slaughter us both. . . . You're putting the slaughterer's blade to your own throat. . . . Yossi, my treasure! Yossi, have a heart."

Yossi just kept stroking the dogs. One of the dogs was tall and reached up to his knee, while the other, short and heavy, curled at his heels, licking Yossi's toes. The deep silence was broken only by the swaying poplars.

Once again, Dobbe screamed:

"Yossi Ber, for pity's sake, come to your senses. The whole village has left. . . . For heaven's sake! Save your life! . . ."

Yossi withdrew from the dogs, who had suddenly started growling at Dobbe.

"I'm not going to run away, Dobbe," his lips barely stammered from under his elfish beard. "I'm not going to run away, I'm not going to run away."

"Master of the Universe! Yossi Ber, what's wrong with you? The Germans will kill us. . . . Are you out of your senses, Yossi Ber? . . . My dearest!"

"I'm not leaving this spot, Dobbe! A human being can't run away from his fate."

The two of them continued standing in the middle of the

room. The smoking kerosene lamp flickered. From the darkness outside they heard the wind blowing through the swaying branches of the poplars. The black shawl of night wrapped the surrounding fields where pasture grass and chamomile were growing; the last stars disappeared from the sky spotted with flame-reddened clouds.

Morning dawned on the village of Dolny-Yary. A group of ethnic Germans was loitering on the sandy road. The first one to step out of the group was short and heavyset, with a yellowish complexion and watery gray eyes. He could barely stand. His body was stubby, and his short squat legs were nestled in a pair of comfortable high boots. He was wearing a green hat, and his yellow face was bathed in greasy sweat. The rest of the crowd carried Jaeger guns slung over their bony shoulders. These German peasants who had watched the panic were now waiting for their countrymen to arrive.

Yossi Ber stood in the middle of the gang, barefoot and hatless, his red beard disheveled, his hair messed up. His feet, with their thin white peasant heels, protruded underneath his black Sabbath coat. His eyes, fixed on the ground, stared at the dusty boots around him. He remained silent. His shirt was open, exposing his bare chest with its red hair. The person wearing the green hat told Yossi Ber to dance a Jewish dance on one foot. Yossi Ber did not understand the language. He stood there saying nothing. The person with the hat gestured to show Yossi Ber what he meant. The rest of the Germans formed a circle. Soon the Jew would have to dance. He will dance. He will dance. . . .

The Germans drew long thin bayonets out of their boots and affixed them to their rifles. They started jabbing the Jew's bare feet with the points of their bayonets. Yossi Ber started hopping on one foot and then the other. A thin ribbon of blood appeared on his left foot. The blood flowed into the sand, staining it red.

Yossi Ber danced.

He danced on one foot, cautiously, fearfully. The long coat got in his way, so he gathered it up with one hand and danced faster, more wildly, with his other hand raised high, spinning like a windmill. Growing tired, he lowered his other leg and danced on it. Now the blood started flowing from his right leg, a warm streamlet flowing freely. The gang guffawed with demonic laughter. Yossi Ber danced to the stabs of bayonets. Left! Right! Left! Right! And the whole time the thugs kept stabbing his dancing feet. His head swayed, as did his disheveled red beard, as if his throat had been slit. A pungent sweat ran down his forehead into his open mouth. He whirled ever more wildly, with ever more stubborn determination. From under his half-shut eyes he saw everything whirling around him. The tall thin poplars beside the path, the stones on the side of the road, the wooden fences, the little houses, the empty highway leading to the Varta, the sky and the sun, all were whirling with him. The whole of Dolny-Yary whirled along with him, and now the blue forests that extended without end, the open fields and the ponds, the thin silvery wind-blown clouds, all joined in the dance.

Although it was midday the stars suddenly appeared. The moon peeped out pale and trembling and twirled with the stars in a dizzying dance with the poplars and the ponds. A song wafted down from the clouds and Yossi Ber heard his father singing to him. His father bent over him and whispered: "Yossi Ber . . . Yossi Ber . . . Dance! Dance . . . Dance, my son, Dance! . . ." His father's melody harmonized with the song emanating from the white stones, the sand, the poplars, the stables and fences, while the swelling sun framed Dolny-Yary like a golden bowl.

For two days Dobbe lay in the cellar with both dogs, constantly stuffing cold meat into their mouths to keep them from lunging out into the open. The whole time the dogs kept surging, while Dobbe lay there on top of them like a corpse. The only light came from a gloomy ray that leaked through a small opening in the cellar.

It was not till the second day that Dobbe decided to leave her hiding place.

Dolny-Yary was deserted. Household goods and discarded old clothes were scattered across the sandy path. Emptiness echoed from every yard, and from time to time Dobbe's shouts rattled around that waste:

"Yossi Ber! Yossi Ber! . . ."

The emptiness of the village answered her, echoing her voice across the blue, mossy forests.

The dogs ran ahead of her. They ran to the path that sloped down the hill, with Dobbe chasing after them. She saw them clinging to a little mound. Drawing closer to the dogs, Dobbe became aware of their outstretched necks and their snouts buried in their forepaws, a canine sadness in their eyes. Each one lay on a side of the mound, as if poisoned.

The gray waters of the Varta flowed on, not far from the mound. The sun sinking beneath the rim of the forests poured an unending web of red and blue tasseled kerchiefs across the void. At last Dobbe was lying on top of the bit of disturbed earth. A patch of black coat peeped out of the little mound and fluttered in the autumn wind like an amputated wing atop the little hill of yellow sand.

Łódź Ghetto, 1940

✦

In the Dark

The brittle winter air was dotted with falling snow, and, as was usually the case on winter nights following the Sabbath, no one was to be seen in the street. Stores and shops were locked and barred. A path had been tramped into the fresh snow by the footsteps of the first and second parties of Jews who had passed through the street earlier that night. The first party had arrived about midnight, the second a little after that, and they were expecting the third to be here before dawn. The light of the electric lamps, which hung over the middle of the street at close intervals, pierced the thin winter air, tinting it red. The entire city seemed in a stupor. A few of the houses—silent in their mission of concealment—entombed the few remaining Jews within their walls. The street was empty except for the swaying electric lamps bent by the wind till they resembled parentheses enclosing only the frigid air of a winter night.

In the courtyard, the small band of Jews, shivering in their short light jackets, pressed against the gate as they waited for the third party of Jews to show up. Already, there were almost enough of them, all wearing their yellow armbands, to make up a prayer quorum. The eldest of the assemblage was Reb Bunem Feitlovitsch, a Jew with a short, trimmed beard resembling the goatee of King George V of England, except that it had been disheveled by the wind. Every now and then he would shuffle out the gate, look as far down the street as he could, and then pull his head back with a sigh. The Jews had been standing here all night, exposed to the wind that blew through their flimsy jackets, chilling them to the bone. They impatiently awaited the arrival of the third group of Jews coming from the city.

The stillness of the night was broken by the windblown screeching of wagon wheels on the peasant trail leading to the gate, an indication that the third party of Jews was coming. The Jew with the George V beard went out the gate again and looked down the street intently for a long time. In the distance, where the street began, a shapeless dark mass could be seen lurching slowly toward the gate. The Jews inside the gate heard footsteps in the snow and the rhythmic beat of steel-reinforced boots pounding the sidewalk. As the sound of the footsteps came closer, the waiting Jews stepped outside the gate and stood in the middle of the road. That was how the rendezvous had been arranged: the Germans would herd the Jewish evacuees up to the edge of the old city and would then turn them over to the eldest of the Jews.

Reb Bunem Feitlovitsch and the small band of Jews waited.

The huge black mass steadily drew closer. Now it was possible to see the outlines of individual human beings carrying bundles. German soldiers in greenish uniforms marched alongside. The cold steel of naked bayonets affixed to rifles reflected the dim light.

Reb Bunem Feitlovitsch stepped out to meet the third party. One of the Germans leading the Jews to the ghetto confronted him. He was short and stocky, wearing a stiff green uniform and a small hat with a skull and crossbones on the tip. His eyelashes were covered with snow, and he reeked of beer and stale cigarettes. Several soldiers advanced and lined up on either side of him. By now, Reb Bunem had drifted pretty far from the gate, and the little group of Jews with yellow armbands had come up behind him. Their knees trembling with fright, they stood there as if they were frozen to the ground. The German looked at Reb Bunem in the darkness and suddenly broke into raucous laughter:

"Ha-ha-ha! . . . Haw-haw-haw!"

He shifted his hat to the other side of his head and looked even more intently at the Jew's face, drawing closer until their noses almost touched. Reb Bunem Feitlovitsch didn't know what to do. He removed the cap from his head. The Jews behind him did likewise. They stood there bareheaded, while a dusting of snow kept falling.

The German mumbled:

"Well, well . . . Are you in charge of this pile of shit? W-e-l-l?"

"Yes, sir," Reb Bunem stammered meekly, as he pointed to the Jews clustered behind him.

The German broke into another paroxysm of laughter. The "haw-haw-haw" burst from the middle of the street and hung over the heads of the little group like a long dull knife.

"Are you the one? You—the King of England?"

Reb Bunem didn't know what to answer. The other puffed steamy vapor right into his face.

The German grabbed Reb Bunem's chin and shook it violently:

"Well, say something. . . ." In his drunken rage, he kept shaking him. "Are you the one? Are you the King of England or not?"

Trembling, Reb Bunem bowed his head.

"No, my dear Sir, my name is Bunem Feitlovitsch, the eldest of the Jews . . . Kaufman . . ."

"Well, well," the German interrupted. "I know all that already. Kaufman . . . Yes, yes! But you're the English king, you swine!"

He punched Reb Bunem in the face with his fist.

Reb Bunem Feitlovitsch shrieked. He felt warm fluid running down his chin. It started dripping into the snow. Drops of blood congealed on the grayish hairs of Reb Bunem's beard.

"And now hurry up and get your Jews moving, English king, and tell them to sing Psalms . . . to Jehovah!"

The German stepped back and whistled to the troops behind him.

The people making up the third party of Jews, who had just arrived, were the first to move.

The human mass shifted like a tangled clump of twisted old rotted tree roots with living black limbs. The injured and the lame shuffled across the snow like a clump of shadows inseparably glued together. For the entire trip, the bizarre congregation had kept its misery in check, stifling even the least hint of a groan so as not to provoke those who were herding them. They marched every step of the way with the unuttered words on their tongues: "Jews, Jews, save us!" And now they were terrified that the hell they had just been through might begin all over again. The winter night was giving way to the grayish stripes of dawn. But it was still too dark to make out individual faces. The snow covered their heads, their shoulders, and the packs of bedding they carried on their backs. Reb Bunem was leading the new arrivals. His head was still covered, and his beard was reddened by blood still pouring from his split lip. The Jew seemed to be leading an entire people into exile.

While the group was being led into the synagogue, Jewish women were cooking and setting out cups of hot coffee in a nearby courtyard. People exhausted from lack of sleep were running around the synagogue, carrying cups of coffee for the newcomers. A collective "Praise the Lord!" burst from their sorrowful souls, a Jewish cry of relief. Those who had just arrived with the third party lay on their packs of bedding like cadavers, some with ears torn off, others with broken arms, battered foreheads, hollow eye sockets. Beneath their swollen eyelids swam visions of what they had been forced to live through the past few hours. Their fainting hearts yearned to return just one more time to the luster of the Jewish dwellings they had just left. In the mind's eye they could see their old Jewish homes, with floors and shelves, walls and windows, chandeliers and landscape paintings, closets, beds, tables, chairs, and glassware. Spectral memories of the homes they had left behind tormented these Jews, who were more dead than alive. Thoughts of their forsaken houses, streets, stairs, porches kept spinning in their heads. Lying here, on their snow-covered packs of bedding, in the dark synagogue, they could not help dreaming of the homes they had abandoned on the opposite side of the city: ruined, forlorn, disgraced.

Reb Bunem Feitlovitsch gathered a quorum and had them commence the morning prayers. He himself went to a washstand and started washing the congealed blood from his beard. The hairs were stuck together like entwined strands of wire, and he was unable to wash away the frozen drops of blood.

Meanwhile, in the darkness, the others had begun to recite portions of the psalms, reading from prayer books they had managed to save, which they now started pulling out of the packs of bedding. They groaned and wept large hot Jewish tears. His reddened beard still dripping, Reb Bunem joined the other Jews. His heart was not receptive to the impassioned verses of the psalms, whose meaning now seemed remote. Before he could open his mouth to join the congregation, the words the drunken German had shouted at him in the street pelted him like a storm of hailstones: "And now sing Psalms to your Jehovah!" For a moment, Reb Bunem was paralyzed, overcome by shame and nausea. The blood rushed from his heart into his hands, which began to tremble. His eyes flashed an uncanny green flame. With a surge of preternatural strength, he suddenly turned to the praying Jews and started ripping the prayer books from their hands. The frightened Jews moved off to the side while Reb Bunem continued tearing the Psalm books from their grasp and casting imprecations on their heads. He shouted with the voice of one possessed, while in the darkness of the synagogue his beet-red face glowed with divine wrath:

"Jews!!! Stop reciting Psalms!!! God is on the side of our enemy! . . . God is with the Germans! . . . I beseech you, recite no more Psalms! . . . Our world is shrouded in darkness!"

As he rattled on in a distraught voice, confusion started to spread through the darkened synagogue. One of the Jews grabbed him from behind, and with all his strength managed to drag him to a bench. Meanwhile, someone doused Reb Bunem's face with cold water. Women started wailing loudly, as Reb Bunem lay stretched on the bench gasping for air. Several men surrounded him and applied ice-cold compresses to his forehead. He lay on the bench with his eyes shut, clutching a torn Psalm book spotted with blood.

Outside, in the little synagogue courtyard, it was still pitch black. On the other side of town, a sickly winter sun blushing with shame was just beginning to rise.

1941

❖

The Death of Anna Nikolayevna Temkin

A strip of cloth hung slackly around his scrawny neck and ran all the way down his chest.

It was a bizarre spectacle. I would not have imagined that such a thing could exist. In truth, the strangeness of the entire chain of events was a bit horrible, and even now, as I tell you the story, I can't shake the pall it casts over my spirit. Somehow, I have the feeling that what happened could not possibly have taken place. And yet . . .

In my daily wanderings through the streets of the ghetto (rain or shine, I never missed a day), I once saw him in a little side street. There was once a grand estate on that street, but now the street was cluttered with rubble—scattered bricks and scraps of old furniture. I say I first saw him, because at first glance you sensed the image of a man: a long baggy man's coat hanging over a pair of emaciated arms, and a pair of naked feet protruding from under that long coat. The hair was a bit long and stuffed into the collar of the overcoat. The face was drawn and pasty, colorless, like the faces of people who spend their nights in abandoned hallways, in some hole in the ground, in a crack in a wall, or maybe just leaning against a fence. But when I looked more closely, my first impression dissipated and I was sure it was a woman, a very gaunt woman, nothing but skin and bone. The coat covered her flat withered breasts, and the roundness of a woman's body had disappeared under the massive breadth of the man's coat.

It was a woman, all right. It was none other than Anna Nikolayevna Temkin.

Unfortunately, I can't tell you much about the origins of Anna Nikolayevna Temkin, because I myself, you should know, don't come from the gentry. On the contrary, my family origins are quite humble. We are plain folk. In his youth my grandfather was a forester but he later gave up that occupation, I don't really know why, and spent the rest of his life—along with his sons and daughters—spinning on a spinning wheel. My father, likewise, didn't wander far from his father's humble trade. He was a weaver in his youth and afterwards supported me, the eldest, and the rest of the children, by manufacturing little cardboard wallets that he sold to storekeepers. Those were very hard times for us. My other grandfather, who came from a very pious family, was a saintly man who spent all his time reciting psalms and died at the age of ninety-three, the Book of Psalms on his bed. But I know this is all beside the point. I just want to make it clear that someone like Anna Nikolayevna Temkin was very far from my own family background, and whatever I say about Anna Nikolayevna Temkin must be the simple truth, because I'm not the only one who knows her story.

On May 1, 1940, the day they sealed the ghetto, making it illegal for the Jews who had been herded there to leave, Anna Nikolayevna Temkin, carrying a small package under her arm, was walking in one of the little ghetto streets. She was supported by a cane with a silver knob, which had belonged to her late husband, Jacob Simon Temkin, who had died about a month earlier in one of the ghetto hospitals. Anna Nikolayevna had gone to stay with a relative who, like tens of thousands of other Jews, hadn't had the sense to escape; now they were all stuck in the narrow, dark streets of the ghetto.

Nestling the package, which was wrapped in a black silk shawl, under her cape, Anna Nikolayevna Temkin was on her way to the merchant, Sergei Semyonovitch. Anna Nikolayevna Temkin was wearing a gold pince-nez and a green chiffon hat with a black veil that reached down to the tip of her nose, so that it covered half her face. As she walked, she tapped the protruding stones with the cane, and every time she encountered someone, she would stop and ask:

"*Izvinitye Gospodin*, do me a favor, uncle [she used to speak Russian and then immediately translate into Lithuanian Yiddish], where is Krutke Alley?"

"Well, take a look at the fine lady who honors us with her presence!" was the angry answer she got from a man with an empty pot in his hand. "I'm glad to see you find our neighborhood so much to your liking now. When did such a grand lady ever come here before? Did she ever come to see how her own brothers and sisters were living? Huh? Never. You could have gone a whole lifetime. But now! To hell with the whole pack of them. They always lived high on the hog up there in their swell places, and you could never get anywhere near them. The high fancy doors were always locked, and in front of the gate was the goy, may he be cursed. But now? A hearty welcome to you! *Izvinitye Gospodin,*" he says, mimicking Anna Nikolayevna's voice, "*Gdye* is Krutke Alley? Blast them all to damn hell!"

The Jew with the empty pot turned aside and spit, leaving her there drenched in his torrent of invective.

Anna Nikolayevna continued on her way, tapping the black cane on the stones. The pince-nez slid down to the end of the chain and bounced on her chest as she walked.

"Granny"—she had stopped a young girl with disheveled braids and a pair of round powdered cheeks—"you want to get to Krutke Alley, do you?"

Anna Nikolayevna takes hold of the pince-nez, lifts her veil a little, puts them to her shortsighted eyes, and looks the girl over.

"*Da, da, varishnya* [Yes, yes, young lady], to Krutke Alley."

"Ha, ha, ha," the girl laughs, her wide-open mouth revealing large teeth, set unsteadily in red gums. "Granny, you probably mean Prevetn Street."

"*Tshto vi skazalyi?* What are you saying? Prevetn Street?"

"Yes, yes, Granny, that's what it really is. Good. Please give me your hand. Do you see that little staircase? About ten steps past that staircase you'll find your Krutke Alley. It's not far from there. If you'd like, I can take you there."

"*Pozhaliste varishnya*, with the greatest pleasure," the old woman said, cheering up measurably. "One sees immediately that you're one of our people. . . ."

The girl, who had been working the street all morning without attracting a single "guest," attached herself to the elderly lady in the green hat, the cape, and pince-nez, as if they were lifelong companions. The girl took her by the arm and led her along the way.

"Who're you visiting, Granny? I know everybody on Krutke Alley."

"*Da?*" Anna Nikolayevna asked. She actually stuttered out of pure joy. "Are you perhaps acquainted with the merchant, Sergei Semyonovitch?"

"Sergei Semyonovitch?" The girl pursed her lips and wrinkled her brow. "Isn't he a tall man with a bald head?"

Anna Nikolayevna Temkin burst into laughter:

"Ha, ha, ha. What would Sergei Semyonovitch be doing with a bald head? *Tshto,* what are you saying? Sergei Semyonovitch and a bald head! *Varishnya,*" she said, turning to the girl, "I see you don't know everybody on Krutke Alley. I'll ask someone else. I have a notebook with me. *Pozhalista,* would you be kind enough, *varishnya,* to hold my package for a minute?"

"With the greatest pleasure, Granny." The girl stopped in her tracks.

She took the package as Anna Nikolayevna put the cane under her arm and started searching through her pocket.

The girl squeezed the package with her fleshy hands, trying to figure out what was in it.

"The old witch has some kind of hard, heavy things in here," she thought. "Who knows what kinds of things an old witch like her might have: jewelry, bracelets, diamonds, maybe gold or silver?"

Anna Nikolayevna read out of a notebook: "Sergei Semyonovitch. Krutke Alley 5/7."

"What?" the young girl shouted joyfully. "Sergei Semyonovitch of 5/7! So I do know him! That's him: a short guy with a flattened nose and long sideburns. Isn't that the guy?"

"That's him, *varishnya,* he's the one all right. They told me to go to him. We're going to do some business. Is it far to go yet to Sergei Semyonovitch?"

The girl had finally figured it out: the merchant Sergei Semyonovitch was actually "Pesach Mamele" of Prevetn Street.

This wasn't the first time that "Pesach Mamele," the notorious con man, had played the role of a rich Russian merchant. For years "Pesach Mamele" had been running a house of ill repute. Now the girl understood that it must be the real stuff in the package. When the merchants and manufacturers had been forced into the ghetto, all the girls started figuring there would be opportunities to make a quick killing. When they were herded into the ghetto, the rich brought with them whatever wealth they were able to conceal and hang on to: jewelry, diamonds, and other precious stones. Clutching the package to her breast, the girl actually started trembling. She took Anna Nikolayevna by the arm and whispered softly to her:

"You know what I'm going to tell you, Granny? We'd better walk a little faster, because who knows whether we'll find Sergei Semyonovitch still alive."

"God save you, you must be joking, *varishnya*," Anna Nikolayevna retorted. "We saw Sergei Semyonovitch just yesterday, Tuesday. He was healthy as a horse."

On the spur of the moment, the girl made up a story about how Sergei Semyonovitch, a very honest and distinguished merchant, had installed himself in the middle of Krutke Alley yesterday and started distributing alms to anyone who approached him. Since there was no shortage of paupers, he gave away money left and right. What can you say? That's just the kind of person Sergei Semyonovitch is, truly one of those Russian souls with a soft heart always open to the plight of the poor. So there he was, Sergei Semyonovitch, standing there dishing out alms. Out of nowhere, a stranger comes up to him (no one knows who) and says to him: "Sergei Semyonovitch, do you know that your mother died?" When he hears this, our Sergei Semyonovitch just collapses, right on the spot, and has to be carried straight to bed.

"And how is Sergei Semyonovitch feeling now?" asks Anna Nikolayevna, with real alarm in her eyes.

"Don't ask, Granny," the girl sighs, with a peculiar expression on her face, and seeing one of her cronies standing at the gate, she passes her the package in the blink of an eye. "Don't ask Granny," she goes on, without pause. "Sergei Semyonovitch is lying on his death bed. He is dying, Sergei Semyonovitch, such a radiant soul. Such a kind Russian heart . . . such a . . ."

As Anna Nikolayevna and the girl reach the house, number

5/7, the girl is extremely agitated. Several disheveled women with their dresses pulled up above their knees are sitting on the stairs, warming their pale sagging flesh in the winter sun.

"*Varishnya*," Anna Nikolayevna calls out, "would you be so kind as to give me my package. We're almost there."

The girl opens her innocent eyes wide with dismay:

"What? Did you say something, Granny?"

Anna Nikolayevna lifts her veil and lowers her pince-nez, as she does when she is about to speak.

"Would you please give me the package, *varishnya*, the package," she repeats, as her aged hands start trembling.

The girl stops in her tracks.

"What package, Granny? Did you have a package?"

Anna Nikolayevna goes pale and shoves the veil up over her green hat.

"Gevald!" she cries out. "The package! The package!"

In a flash, the girl with the round cheeks has disappeared.

For a moment, Anna Nikolayevna is on the verge of fainting. Completely distraught, she starts running up and down the sidewalk brandishing the black cane with its silver knob, and trying, unsuccessfully, to put on her pince-nez. The old woman is convulsed with sobs. The green hat sways on her head like a parrot. Underneath Anna Nikolayevna's cape, her shoulders heave in uncontrollable spasms.

The women on the stoop just look at her. Anna Nikolayevna walks over to them:

"I beg you, have mercy, *varishnyes*. Would you be so kind as to show me the dwelling of Sergei Semyonovitch!"

"Which Sergei Semyonovitch might that be, Granny?"

"The merchant, Sergei Semyonovitch, who is dying right now."

The women look at her more closely.

"Sergei Semyonovitch who is dying right now?"

"Sergei Semyonovitch who is dying right now!"

"May every demon of the night haunt your every sleep, Granny," shouts a brash redhead. "If you're a nut-case go to the nuthouse."

"*Izvoltye, varishnya*," Anna Nikolayevna implores, tears in her eyes, as she grabs the redhead's hand. "The merchant Sergei

Semyonovitch, the one who was distributing alms yesterday, right in the middle of this street. Today he is dying. . . ."

"Foo! That's all I need is a disgusting witch like you!"

Anna Nikolayevna collapsed in a dead faint.

By the time they had brought her to and got her back onto the street, Anna Nikolayevna no longer had her green hat, no longer had her cane with the silver knob, no longer had her cape, her pince-nez, her shoes. Anna Nikolayevna now stood in the middle of the street barefoot, clad in her undergarments, her disheveled gray hair blowing in the breeze. She did not know where to go next. She peered about with her shortsighted eyes. A street urchin took her by the hand and began to lead her. Soon a crowd of children had gathered behind her and escorted her out of Krutke Alley to a chorus of hoots and howls.

After all these happenings, Anna Nikolayevna dropped out of sight for at least three weeks. Where she holed up during this time I don't know. Most likely she had taken up residence in some doorway, or in an abandoned flat, because after being driven out of Krutke Alley she lost her memory, as often happens to elderly people who have experienced a severe shock. All I know is that she finally turned up in an alleyway where some neighborhood folks had brought her and left her.

During the night someone threw her a coat, and dressed in that hand-me-down coat, Anna Nikolayevna gathered herself together and started roaming the ghetto streets, barefoot and nearsighted.

Anna Nikolayevna took to hanging out at the bridge near Holy Mary Church. Dressed in her long coat, and barefoot, the old woman must have crossed that wooden bridge hundreds of times, scouring both sides of the street with her nearsighted eyes, looking for someone below. After crossing, she would shuffle around at the end of the bridge for a while, and then would mingle with the crowd going the other way, returning to the side she had just come from. She would make these round trips tens of times a day, dragging herself along by the railing. Back and forth she would go across the bridge near the Holy Mary Church.

On one occasion, however (no one can say exactly how this happened), the old woman leaned over the railing, and in the blink of an eye the soldier patrolling beneath found the quivering body of a human being impaled on his bayonet.

The startled soldier fell to the ground with the impaled body. Anna Nikolayevna was lying in the middle of the street at the feet of the soldier, with a bayonet in her breast. At first, the soldier shivered with disgust, but he soon pulled himself together and slowly withdrew the bayonet from Anna Nikolayevna's rib cage, the way you would pull a knife out of a loaf of bread.

Every time I happen to pass the bridge near Holy Mary Church in my daily wanderings through the ghetto, I get the notion that among the hundreds of women crossing the bridge I can see the hunched-over emaciated figure of Anna Nikolayevna. Whenever I shuffle past those wooden railings, my heart starts pounding and I look around in search of something. I cross the bridge repeatedly, always looking to see what is down below. Sometimes, I stop near the railing and just stand there. Perhaps I will be granted the good fortune to save a human soul.

✿

In a Death Alley

The young man sitting across from me told the following tale:
It's very possible that if I hadn't received that letter addressed to a relative of mine the entire affair would not have occurred, and the incident I'm going to relate to you would never have seen the light of day. But you know as well as I that everything must have a beginning, and it so happens that the beginning of this story — is the letter.

A letter was left at my address. The letter was written to a relative of mine who lives not far from me. A ten-minute walk. I had to make sure he received his letter, so I decided to deliver it to him that evening.

He lived in an unpaved alley, narrow and winding, like so many of the streets in the ghetto. Old houses resembling the fishermen's huts on Scandinavian embroideries clung to each other, telling the secrets of past generations of Jews and their Jewish practices. The once quaint picket fences around the houses had been dismantled, leaving only isolated boards protruding here and there like long-forgotten grave markers. The few stores that had done business here before the war were fitted with iron bars now rusting from extended exposure to soaking rains. I had an eerie feeling that the abandoned narrow alley merged with a dead-end street that led to an ancient cemetery; I don't know how to explain it, but that alley eventually did lead to a forsaken burial ground.

I couldn't spot a single face looking out of the crooked windows lining the street; the eaves hung low to the ground, tearful and silent. As I passed by an open corridor, a putrid wind blew a moldy stench into my nostrils. It seemed to me as though everyone in that place was already dead, and that the corpses were just

24

waiting to be taken away. But since no one had come to this particular street to pick up the dead, they just remained there in dark rooms as the wind wafted a stale stench of decaying Jewish bodies across the alley. The black wagons that collected the corpses from the houses came here only infrequently, and even they preferred to park on a side street and wait for the young boys to bring the corpses to them through the open courtyards. The corpse carriers would run with their quarry as though they were stealing something of value from that street and were afraid to look to the right or left. They hurried as fast as they could, because it often happened that while they were carrying a corpse from that alley the hand of the dead person would suddenly fall dangling from the litter, and then a leg would follow, and then there would be no way they could make it to the wagon. The dead person held them back as if he were reluctant to leave this place, this special death alley.

But that's not what I wanted to tell you. You can see already how that letter to my kinsman led me into what I can only call another world. Just telling you the story from the beginning reminds me of that alley where my relative lived. Anyway, by the time I got there, total darkness had descended, and I was the only person in the alley. Suddenly, it started to rain. Dark clouds galloped across the sky like stampeding wild horses. I could have sworn they were the harnessed beasts that pulled the huge black death-wagons through the ghetto streets.

There was a flash of lightning.

You should know that ever since childhood I've had a fear of lightning. I don't know why, but a storm always throws me into such a panic that I have to find some dark spot where I can hide. When I was still a child I always used to crawl into a cellar, or my mother would take me under her apron and cover my eyes. When I grew up that fear of lightning stayed with me and grew as if it were a part of me, as a hand grows, or a foot.

A flash of lightning sent me sprawling through a ramshackle doorway into a dark corridor. I ventured further inside the house, because the rain had started coming down very hard.

I stood in the hallway and examined my surroundings: the doors on both sides of the corridor were open, but I couldn't see what was happening inside, because, as you know, I'm a bit shortsighted. So I drew closer and looked into one of the apartments:

Inside the first door, a very skinny Jewish woman in a short jacket, who looked for all the world like a crumbling tombstone, was shuffling around the room. She was barefoot, and her swollen ankles looked like a pair of tree stumps. On the floor behind her, two children were climbing on a heap of greens and garbage that had been swept together into a little pile. You think, perhaps, that I'm referring to greens like fresh salad or sweet cabbage that grow in fertile fields outside the ghetto. No, I'm talking about the kinds of greens that come directly from the trash can: sticky leaves, the remains of rotted greens-roots, and slimy potato peels. . . . You know the kind of thing I'm talking about. The woman was bustling at the side of a bed, and it seemed to me that someone was lying in the bed. She shouted at the children constantly, things like:

"Sheindele, don't put that into your mouth. . . . It'll make you sick. . . . Berele, don't scavenge through the garbage. . . . Dysentery . . ."

But Sheindele already had something in her mouth and was chewing on it.

"Mommy," Berele yelled to her. "Mommy, Mommy, Sheindele ate a turd. . . ."

You laugh? You think perhaps that I'm telling you something I just made up out of thin air? God forbid I should make up such stories. . . . What, what . . . But it's not just since yesterday you've known me. I wouldn't tell you lies. You know that.

Suddenly the woman noticed me standing at the open door.

"Who you looking for?" she asked, her voice sounding like an echo from a hollow tin pot.

"Uh, no one," I answered. "I'm just waiting for the rain to stop."

I moved a little away from the doorway.

There was another flash of lightning, and at that moment the room was illuminated by a green light. In that instant of illumination I saw that someone was indeed lying in the bed, someone fully clothed. The person's face was yellow as wax, and he had a thin scraggly beard like the one you sometimes see on Jesus

Christ in religious paintings. His hands, which looked like a pair of yellow candles, rested on the coat that covered him. I couldn't see any more than that, because, after all, how long does a flash of lightning last? And that corner of the room quickly returned to darkness.

"Shimmele," I heard the old woman call out. "Ya gonna eat some soup? A curse on me and on your orphans . . . Have some soup, Shimmele. . . . The doctor said that today you're supposed to feel better. . . . 'Sentery can't last that long. Ya'll see. Ya gotta get better. . . ."

"Dysentery, yet," I thought, and moved a little further from the doorway. But still, he was a human being, so I just said, casually turning into the room:

"Tell me, I beg you, why didn't you send your husband to the hospital?"

"Send him?" she hissed bitterly, mocking my words. "It's easy for you to say, 'Send him.' I ran around for three weeks. 'Gevald,' I yelled at them. 'He's dying on me. . . . Whole buckets are pouring out of him. . . .' So they say: 'Ain't no room.' I say: 'Waddaya mean, no room?' They say: 'D'ya think you're the only one? There's no room, and that's all there is to it. . . .' At least if he had something he could lie on . . . Well. . . . His whole back ain't nothin' but a bunch of sores. . . . There ain't even no straw mattress. . . . Not even no straw . . ."

By this time I decided not to wait for the next flash of lightning.

I moved further inside the corridor.

The door of the next apartment opened into a small narrow room cluttered with strange furniture, and no bed. Inside, there was only silence. An open flat with not a person in it. That struck me as odd. I stuck my head into the room, purely out of curiosity. Then I heard someone shouting from one of the dark corners of the room:

"Who you looking for?"

"Uh," I answered. "No one. I'm waiting for the rain to stop."

"And when someone's waiting for the rain to stop," answered the voice from the darkness, "does he stick his nose into a stranger's flat?"

"Excuse me," I said. "I thought no one was here."

"What do you mean, no one here? It's already the fourth day that I haven't moved from this spot. . . . Three more days—and the *shiva* will be over. . . ."*

A streak of lightning cut through the night. Only at this moment did I realize that the voice was coming right off the floor. A deformed female body was sitting on a footstool.

"For whom are you sitting *shiva*," I asked.

"It's about time we were sitting *shiva* for the enemies of the Children of Israel," she gasped. "Could we have imagined such a catastrophe? But that's how it's been willed. . . . He Who is in heaven knows what He is doing. . . . His ways are hidden from the eyes of men."

"Dysentery?" I asked.

"What else? D'ya think he's complaining of a tasty roast? Ain't half the courtyard already gone, thanks mercy, to their 'liverance? Why not? Who ain't? The weaver's two daughters . . . The Litvak and his wife, the cobbler's little girl . . . Shprintze and Zlate from across the way . . . And now, along with the rest of them, Shimmele. How long can he last? Is it any wonder? What people eat—you shouldn't know from it. It turns your guts to water. . . . And when you die already, praise the Lord, you can't even bury the corpse right. There ain't anyone to bury it. . . . My Zalman, may he forgive me, laid a week on the bare floor waitin' for the burial crew. . . . Where ya gonna find them? Didn't everyone leave in that winter of burning, when they burned every last stick of furniture for heat and cooking? And even a little straw to lift the carcass on, you think we got any? Also not. If not them up there we wouldn't even have a bit of straw. . . ."

I saw there would be no end to this diatribe. When a gossip starts blabbering . . . Well, you know what it's like. . . . Nonetheless, seeing that it was still raining, I thought: "How can I go out in this rain? My relative will just have to wait for his letter."

"What do you mean?" I asked her. Are you telling me there's not a straw mattress in the entire house? There's no place you can get some straw for a corpse?"

---

* Shiva is the ritual of the first seven days of mourning.

"He-he-he," the old woman laughed at me, toothlessly. "Sure there ain't none. And do you think there's even a whole bed here? When my Zalman died, who do you think gave us a little bit of straw?"

"Not the ones up there?"

"Sure they did. And who do you think gave a bit of straw to the Litvak? Also them. Really. The ones up there. In the whole house there ain't a mattress with straw, only up there, by the divorced lady. . . ."

Just as I was about to ask whom she was referring to, there was a powerful flash of lightning and bolt of thunder that caused the whole house to shake. I actually leapt up from the doorway, and as I did so I bumped into some strange person who had been standing behind the stairs. It had now grown completely dark, so I became somewhat frightened. That same moment, I felt someone whispering close to my ear:

"Perhaps you would like to come to my place. I live alone. . . . Here, upstairs."

You've known me a long time, and you know I'm not one of those people whose feelings are easily moved. But that whispering from behind the stairs by some strange woman, whose face I couldn't see, whose shadow was not even visible, just that whispering in the dark—it caused me to quake in my boots. . . . I know the whole thing sounds weird, but I've undertaken to convey the truth to you, even if it makes you take me for some sort of an eccentric. . . . I'm not just making up some wild story—that's not my way. But this is exactly what I saw: in one doorway a person in death throes, in the second a woman sitting *shiva*, and who knows in how many of the flats in that death-house there were people dying. And all that had made no impression on me, as if I had seen nothing unusual. So there I am, standing under the stairway when a warm feminine hand leads me by the arm up the stairs into a warm uneasy darkness.

The stairs we climb are not ordinary stairs that ascend one step after another. No. You step onto a stair—and immediately there is a wide gap before you get to the next stair, and it continues that way to the very top. On my way up I almost fell into an abyss. The woman went up ahead of me, and every second I would stumble and my hands would grab the thick flesh of her thighs. In the darkness I could tell that she must have shapely, pretty legs.

Finally, we made it to the top. I walked through an open door. It was completely dark inside, so I didn't have to shield my eyes, as is usual in such circumstances. . . . In the dimness I could make out a round bundle curled up in the middle of the room, which cried out in a shrill voice: "Leibele, my crown . . . Leibele . . ."

I felt a chill clutch my heart: "My God, what have I blundered into here? . . . I'm in a house where everyone is dying."

"Everyone in this house is dying," I said aloud, not knowing what else to say.

The room was lighted by a little candle propped up on the table. In the dim light, I saw only a high bed and a thick sack of straw covered with a sheet. Long yellow straws resembling ritual fringes were sticking out of the sides. . . .

Now, for the first time, I noticed a short figure, still heavy with sleep, lift itself from that bed.

My guide spoke up behind me:

"Blimmele, please go to a neighbor's place for a few minutes. Our guest is shy. . . ."

"You can draw the curtain. . . . What is he, then, some kind of a bumpkin?" the hunched-over shade answered crossly.

Blimmele leaves. The curtain is pulled.

As I stood there, a naked arm embraced me. I just kept standing there, totally confused. The sight of the stuffed straw mattress filled me with a strange sense of terror. Suddenly, I heard the door burst open, the curtain was pulled away, and a man with a long beard stuck his head inside:

"Excuse me, young man, can you come downstairs for a little while? . . . We need you to help lift a corpse. . . ." Blimmele, who was right behind the man, shouted over his head:

"Rosy, give the young man some straw to take with him. . . . From the sack of straw. Shimmele's gone to his rest. . . ."

I grabbed my jacket and ran out of that room like a whirlwind.

If you had seen me running from that house, you would surely have said: "It's a spirit leaving, not a human being."

"But what happened to the letter to your relative? Did you ever deliver the letter?" I ask the young man sitting opposite me. The sweat is streaming down his face.

"*The letter? Is that what you're asking about? Here it is. It's been lying in my pocket for three months, now. . . . Who knows if I'll ever deliver it? I'm scared to return to that strange death alley.*"

1941

✤

The Workbench

Including the five years he had labored for Black Hersh, Sanele had worked at the loom for almost forty years. Actually, you couldn't really count the first five years as serious work because, as everyone knows, an apprentice to a stranger—especially an apprentice training to become a weaver—does everything in the world except the very things that might open the beginner's eyes to the foggy secrets of the weaver's trade. He runs errands for the old weavers, bringing them packages of cigarettes; he helps the boss's wife wash the kitchen floor, peel potatoes, carry buckets of water; he even helps make sauerkraut. He might even be asked to hold the baby wrapped in swaddling a couple of hours a day. And by some miracle he might even get to stand in an unobtrusive spot and watch the old weavers "shoot," so he can learn the trade. But that doesn't happen very often, because, after all, when does an apprentice have a free moment without anything to do but watch the weavers "shoot"? The craft of weaving has to seep into the apprentice's head on its own, just by his hanging out in the weaving room, sweeping up the fine wool from the scissors, or helping to turn the roller on the loom.

The trade was usually handed down from generation to generation of Jewish weavers in the narrow smoke-filled rooms of Balut; everybody on the weavers' street went through those initial apprenticeship years, and then each one became a weaver himself, with his own loom. Jewish children started apprenticing, to learn the basics of the weaver's trade.

Sanele was short and stocky, with a flat face dark as ink. But though he was puny, he had five sons who were sturdy as oaks. The sons had their father's flat face and broad weaver's hands.

There were also some daughters in the household—tall strapping girls who sang sad Yiddish songs as they worked at their spinning wheels. All the daughters still lived at home, for they didn't want to get married. After their mother died, they helped their father run the little factory. Aside from the various looms that banged away in the dark cellarlike rooms, Sanele also contracted work out to a pair of Jewish Balut weavers and to some Germans from the German settlement of Zubordz. Sanele's sons worked at the looms—separating the yarns, rolling the finished fabric from the trees, winding bolts of cloth on spools, and repairing the machinery. For years the daughters toiled at their spinning wheels. On the cellar floor at their feet, innumerable colored spools rolled around like pine cones.

Sanele would not let anybody else deal with the Germans. Those Germans, he used to say—you can't trust the boys to handle them. You've got to know how to deal with the Germans from Zubordz. To be perfectly frank, the work contracted out to the Germans brought in substantial earnings. Father Sanele set up a small office for himself near the window at the far end of the room and would sit there all day, deeply engrossed in his accounts. In a small book he would record the payments received, merchandise delivered, and wages paid out to the subcontractors, all in crabbed shaky Yiddish letters. . . .

Every Friday the Germans came to town to settle their accounts. They came in their wooden clogs, with their pants drawn and tied over the knee-high socks their wives had knitted for them. On their shoulders they carried the finished merchandise. They would sit down on the crates of fabric near the father's office, and the entire time they were there, the girls watched every movement of their hands. It would have been all too easy for one of these Germans to lift the cover off one of the boxes and stuff a fistful of spools into his sack. Sanele would sit in his office settling accounts with the Germans one at a time. While they were waiting, some of the Germans smoked strong German cigarettes made of coarse tobacco, while others stuffed the homegrown weed into long winding pipes; with their village manners they would spit on the floor as they made gurgling noises in their throats. They stole flirtatious glances at Sanele's daughters, who stood with their hands on their ample hips, watching the Germans, who had no idea why the girls were standing around. The Germans would grab the girls by the chin with their coarse hands, and the girls would break out of their grasp and slap their grimy tobacco-stained fingers.

Johann was a German with a bird-face who always tried to speak Yiddish when he came into Sanele's shop. He wore a flat yellowish hat perched on his head like a brass plate. When he came in he would flip the pack of merchandise off his shoulders so that it would always land next to Roch'tche. Then he would take off his flat hat and extend his slimy hand to her. Roch'tche did not stop working at the spinning wheel. She would just let his hand hang there in midair. The German would smile forlornly. Then he would grab her thick hair, braided like a Sabbath loaf and gathered in a bun on her soft neck. Bending over her, he would sigh, blowing his breath, which already reeked of alcohol, right into her face:

"Ai, Roch'tche, Roch'tchele, when you make marry? You girl . . ."

Roch'tche would stop spinning, smooth out her rumpled hair, and say angrily:

"Is it any of your stinking business, Johann fool? . . ."

The rest of the Germans laughed at the goings-on. Thin piercing laughter. Johann laughed with them. The Jews behind the looms stopped their work. Though it was Friday and the pre-Sabbath minutes were slipping away quickly, they placed their hairy weaver's hands on their chests. They were so convulsed with laughter that even the benches they were sitting on seemed to join in. The entire weaving room would reverberate with laughter until Sanele shouted out of his corner:

"Johann! . . . Let me see your merchandise! . . . We'll see how much you've tried to chisel on the weight today! . . ."

Climbing over the crates of finished cloth, the German would sit down next to Sanele in the office and the two of them would start figuring. The rest of the Germans, who had already settled their accounts, waited off to the side. The girls didn't stop watching their hands for a second. Sanele knew what the Germans were waiting for. As soon as Johann's account was settled, Sanele would fling the short coat over his shoulders and go outside.

With the empty sacks under their arms, the Germans would follow him in single file. They all entered the inn run by the widow, and here, in the widow's inn, among plates of soaked chickpeas, cold pilsner beer, and tough chicken livers, Sanele would drink toasts with his Germans till it was time to light Sabbath candles.

By the time Sanele returned, the weaving room had been transformed. Everything scrubbed and sparkling. The spinning wheels had been put away in corners and covered with tablecloths and quilts. The looms were set off to the side and covered. The Sabbath had arrived. Dim and mysterious, the Sabbath floated out of white cellar walls and remote corners as if it had been hiding there all week waiting for that moment when the Friday sun would set, allowing the profane to dissolve into the holy.

The polished yellow candelabra, with its white flickering candles, has been set on the table. The girls are washing their jet black hair in a huge basin and combing it with fine-toothed combs. The boys haven't waited for their father, but have hurried off to prayers without him. As soon as the father gets back from the inn, he shucks off his weekday vest with the paper money stuffed in the pockets and hangs it in the closet. He puts on his Sabbath coat and takes a peek outside. It's too late to go to synagogue, so he finds a spot in a corner of the room, and with his hand resting on the covered loom recites the Sabbath prayers rapidly but with passion.

When her mother, Sarah-Leah, died, Roch'tche was little more than a child, though her siblings were already grown and running the factory. The oldest, Vigder, worked at the loom. Unlike his brothers, he didn't have the temperament to spend most of the day reckoning in the account books, examining the finished merchandise for defects, and shouting at the emaciated loom operators to work faster. That was no work for Vigder. He preferred to sit at the loom on his own and bang away at the batten like the other laborers, and after work he enjoyed reading Yiddish books checked out of the library.

When the father became a widower, the daughters took over management of the household and followed their father around as if he were a sick child. Sanele would sometimes sit down at a loom on one of the workmen's benches and work alongside the laborers. He would toil at the loom for a few days to work off his grief. His children could see that something was gnawing at their father. The other weavers whispered to each other: "Sanele's gone off the deep end. . . ." When the Germans from Zubordz showed up with their packages, the sons had to deal with them. Sanele himself avoided the Germans as much as possible to avoid having to visit the widow's inn. The Germans made up for the few pennies he would have spent on beer and soaked chickpeas by increasing the price they charged for their work.

As the years went by, Sanele's dwelling gradually emptied out. His sons fled to the four winds. Only Roch'tche was left with her father. The sons would visit infrequently. When they did come, they wouldn't say a word the whole time they were there. Then they would leave and not show up again for months.

Sanele would complain to Roch'tche, "How come you don't settle down? The years are flying by." Roch'tche always gave the same answer: "Now that you're alone, Daddy, shall I leave you? Now, when everyone else has abandoned you?"

Sanele couldn't look directly into his daughter's eyes. He dragged the last of the woolen blankets out of the closet and went to the market. When he returned he sat down at the loom where Vigder used to work. It was on that same loom and workbench that Sanele had started working for Black Hersh. That bench had been with Sanele his entire life. How many Jewish weavers had sat on that very bench rocking back and forth as they plied their monotonous trade. The middle of the bench was badly worn and creaked at the least touch. A small amount of unprocessed yarn was left on the warp of the loom, enough for a couple of small bolts. A bittersweet yearning to work at the loom seized Sanele. He impulsively rolled up his sleeves and started a rhythmic loud banging, as in the old days.

Sanele wiped the sweat off his brow. The batten seemed unusually heavy, as if loaded with stones. One more "shot," and the thread would be used up. Roch'tche begs her father not to be foolish and to get away from the loom. But Sanele keeps banging away. A strange yellow color suffuses his drawn face. Seeing his face, Roch'tche is frightened. Hearing the sudden banging of the loom, the neighbors peer into the window. In the blink of an eye they're inside the room. They notice that Sanele is "shooting" without thread. The empty shuttle, with its shiny tip, moves back and forth, back and forth. The neighbors stand around for a while. They look at each other, then tiptoe quietly out of the room while Sanele keeps rocking on the bench.

As soon as the war broke out and the Germans took over, Sanele took to his bed. He had come down with a serious illness. No one even knew what it was. From Sanele's room you could hear what was going on outside: people were running through the streets in panic. Jews were fleeing, going into hiding, running from the city to the countryside. They were afraid to remain in the big city. Something was going to happen very soon. Just yesterday the Polish army had retreated to Warsaw by way of the Brzezin Road. The ethnic Germans of Łódź were already goose-stepping through the streets with swastikas on their lapels. They strutted in groups from one Jewish dwelling to another, plundering along the way. Jews ran away, leaving all their belongings unguarded.

Early in the morning several wagonloads of peasants had rolled into the narrow weaver's street of Balut. Now the wagons were leaving—filled with bedding, women, and children. Frightened weavers shuffled along behind the wagons, shouting at the peasant drivers to speed it up to the highway. But the peasant drivers, who were in no hurry, smoked their pipes, and every now and then would climb slowly down from the wagons to start bargaining all over again.

As Roch'tche was sitting near her sick father, she heard the racket in the courtyard growing louder, as if the whole world were going mad. Jews were dragging packages through the little courtyard. Youths with rucksacks on their shoulders were kissing their mothers goodbye, running quickly out the gate. The mothers stood there, hands clenched in anguish, then sat down at the pump and wept.

Suddenly a silence settled on the courtyard. Some people passed by Sanele's window as Roch'tche plumped up the pillow for her father. Before long a few men with swastikas on their lapels entered the room. One of them walked directly to the bureau, opened the doors wide and demanded money. Roch'tche stood near them, her hands trembling.

Sanele was lying in bed, his eyes half closed. He saw people rummaging around the room and throwing everything out of the bureau. Almost at the same moment a glimmer of hope lit up Sanele's eye and Roch'tche's. The man with the baton in his hand, giving orders to the Germans, somehow looked very familiar. The Fridays of times past crept into a remote corner of consciousness: the account-settling with the Zubordz Germans, the visits to the widow's inn. Suddenly Sanele and Roch'tche shouted, at the same moment:

"Johann, Herr Johann! . . ."

The German was waving his baton in the air. In his high shiny black boots he seemed to take up the whole room.

"The old Johann is gone. Now there is another Johann. Understood?" he shouted at Sanele, and ripped the bedding off him.

Roch'tche pleaded with the German: "Herr Johann. Father's sick. He's been confined to bed for months."

In reply, Johann orders his men to tear the goose-down quilts off Sanele and search the bed because the Jew must have stashed away plenty of money. The quilts are thrown to the floor. Sanele is uncovered and shivering. The German tells him to get out of bed. Roch'tche helps her father out of bed and stands him barefoot on the floor. The Germans ransack the bed. They empty out the bureau but find nothing. Johann is in a fury. As he leaves he brings his thin whip down on Sanele's shirt a few times. A few angry red welts pop up under the shirt, on Sanele's soft flesh.

Roch'tche applies wet sheets to her father's naked swollen body. Little Sanele doesn't open his eyes. Now he sees himself once again behind the loom, sitting on his bench. In his hands the shuttle speeds back and forth as if possessed by a demon. His face is flushed and the veins running through his temples feel like taut hot wires.

After that, the father did not spend much more time in bed. He fell into a sleep from which he would not wake. Roch'tche didn't even make an attempt to call people in and express her grief.

Sanele died like a dog. The few Jews who came running into the room found him stone dead. They lifted him and lay him down on the dark floor next to the loom.

Meanwhile, the Germans had ordered the Jews to nail Jewish stars to their doors. Every day the cemetery was filled with Jewish corpses from the city and Balut. In Sanele's courtyard, two Jews hung themselves. Jewish synagogues in the city were burned.

Before Sanele's funeral a neighbor advised Roch'tche that it would be advisable to bring boards to the cemetery since there was no wood. As her father lay in the wagon, Roch'tche remembered something. She grabbed the bench from the loom at which her father had worked and took it along. Her father did not have to remain in the purification room very long. They sawed the edges of the bench at both ends. It was just the right width for Sanele's narrow childlike body.

Łódź Ghetto, 1941

The Singing of the Birds

The two things in the world Velvel the Redhead cared about were his hurdy-gurdy—a Czech music box—and his flock of pigeons. After the Festival of Tabernacles, when the chilling Polish rains started falling and the windows of the more affluent courtyards had been padded with cotton, Velvel the Redhead would no longer leave the narrow alley. He would tuck the music box into a corner, cover it with a sheet, and then confine the two guinea pigs in a box lined with hay. In addition to his own flock, Velvel the Redhead's "pigeon-roof" was inhabited by a flock of small blackbirds and some gray screeching sparrows who sought to build their nests here. During the blue harvest days, a cheerful twittering of birds echoed under the little window facing the narrow street. The birds filled the air with a bright silvery chirping, joining the haughty pigeons in their flights over the low rooftops. In this way, fall and winter would drag into spring. When the sky above the narrow street finally lifted and the clouds dissipated, then Velvel the Redhead would uncover his music box, take his two guinea pigs out of the hay, and once again set out for the unfriendly courtyards of the city.

This particular year, winter arrived early. Swollen clouds gorged themselves with moisture only to regurgitate it in storms of dark angry snow. Birds disappeared from the rooftops, and the two mangy hounds still being kept by Jews eventually died of starvation. Cats crawled under the barbed wire at night to head for the city. House pets and domesticated birds were no longer to be seen in the ghetto streets. Not a single pigeon remained in Velvel the Redhead's pigeon cage. The two emaciated guinea pigs lay in a pile of stale hay, squealing like hungry mice. A sickly puffiness could now be discerned on the Jews' pallid faces. Meat stripped from dead army horses in Polish fields started to appear in the butcher shops which had had nothing in them for months but congealed blood stains.

Velvel the Redhead spent his days at the window facing the roof, staring aimlessly at the gray winter sky. Every now and then a flock of robins would pass high above the ghetto streets, without bothering to stop. They would fly by with a strange chirping. Sometimes Velvel could discern a small group of pigeons beyond the clouds: wheeling in semicircles, cutting the air sharply, they would eventually descend with a velvet fluttering of their wings, just as his own pigeons once did.

A decree was issued ordering Jews to turn in all musical instruments, those that had been left behind in the ghetto, as well as those that had been brought in recently. Jews streamed from their houses, carrying aged, tearful fiddles that had hung on the walls from time immemorial, instruments that had soothed and comforted Jews in their hour of greatest suffering; large wedding-basses with elongated necks; thin flutes; pot-bellied drums; cymbals, mandolins, harmonicas, and brass trumpets—all of which the Balut entertainers and courtyard musicians had hidden, to be reclaimed after the war. The Jews brought all these instruments to the marketplace, then handed them over to two Germans, who tossed them into a wagon. Those who gave up their instruments did so with unexpressed sadness and grief, but some Jews still kept their fiddles hidden in cellars or attics. When the Germans hauled a black piano from some unknown place on a garbage wagon, the sight of it wounded the Jewish soul to the quick. The ivory keys protruded through the open lid of the piano like the teeth of a dead horse. As the garbage wagon rocked through the streets, a frustrated, despairing groan could sometimes be heard coming from those enormous horse teeth.

Velvel the Redhead woke at the crack of dawn and removed the sheet covering the hurdy-gurdy. Its silken draperies, enlivened by two blond-braided pretty women with naked shoulders, dazzled him. As he placed his hands on the box, a warmth passed through his fingers. He felt an urge to play a Viennese waltz. He slipped the straps over his shoulder, and as he began to crank the erect handle, a soft lilting melody echoed through the room, as if the two women on the silken draperies were singing in some exotic nightclub. Cranking the arm of the hand organ, Velvel the Redhead lifted his head to the sky, as though looking for someone far away. The guinea pigs began to stir in the hay and stuck out their narrow, pointed faces. The melody had awakened them, and they started screeching like demanding children. Even when Velvel the Redhead set out across the little courtyard for the marketplace, the hand-organ slung over his shoulders, they didn't stop.

Stooped under the weight of the music box, Velvel the Redhead shuffled through the little street. He bent his head to the ground, like a horse pulling a heavy load. His feet sank into the soft dark melting snow. Isolated clouds, puffy with the fertile spring already blossoming somewhere in the woods, floated above the rooftops. In the ghetto streets, black ice remained invisible under trampled snow. Velvel the Redhead dragged himself and the music box to the wagon, already overloaded with fiddles. The two Germans had to grab their bulging bellies for laughter when they saw him. They asked him to play something for them on the "shit-box." Velvel the Redhead tossed the hurdy-gurdy across his stomach and gave a flourish with his hand. The Germans perked their ears and squinted, trying to catch the drift of the melody that eased from under the drapery. Suddenly, they sprang up, raised their thin whips, and delivered several lashes to Velvel's face. They paused for a moment, then started lashing his face again. Velvel the Redhead shielded his blood-streaked face with one hand and gesticulated with the other, as the Germans barked:

"You shit—Jewboy . . . How dare you desecrate our gre-at, gre-at Strauss! . . ."

The lashes sent warm rivulets of blood streaming down Velvel the Redhead's face onto the music box. The Germans finally grabbed the box and carefully set it atop the pile of fiddles, as if it were a wounded soldier.

When he returned from the marketplace, Velvel the Redhead collapsed on his iron bed. His face was rutted with bloody trenches. He felt a stickiness on his teeth. A pain exploded inside him, as if a glowing coal had lodged in his throat. He touched his forehead and felt a throbbing behind his eyes. His fingers grew soggy, sticky with blood as he ran them across his tattered face. He needed air. He barely made it to the window and managed to throw it open. A soft breeze blew into the room, like the warm breath of a human being. The distant blue sky was visible again above the roof. Velvel the Redhead stuck his hand out the window and then patted his face, as if he thought he could wash off the congealed blood with air. Suddenly he felt his heart skip a beat: a flock of sparrows had gathered on the little roof, where they warbled incessantly. After many long months they had returned. They hopped about and twittered, filling the air with their silvery chirping. They flew up to the pigeon roost, then onto the roof, and from the roof skipped hurriedly to the open window, hopping and twittering as though they were celebrating some sort of festival. They were not afraid to get close enough to Velvel for the Redhead to see their green and mother-of-pearl eyes. The singing of the birds hung suspended under the pigeon roost and floated over the roof deep into the twilight.

Łódź Ghetto, 1941

Sabbath Candles

To be frank, Itte Binne has lost her ability to discern the fine line dividing truth from fantasy.

In a very short span of time, Itte Binne's family had been exterminated, like so many other Jewish families whose misplaced optimism led them to move, with the meager remnants of their household belongings, into the ghetto. If you had shown Itte Binne an image of her past life, she wouldn't have recognized it, any more than people recognize old photographs of close relatives whose countenances have been eroded by the passing years. The days she had endured in the ghetto had diminished Itte Binne till she felt as if her soul had been locked in an ever-tightening vise.

Strange as it may seem, what pained Itte Binne the most in her bitter ghetto existence was the loss of her old Sabbath candelabra: a tall proud candelabra on slender silver feet, covered with various adornments and carvings. Above all, she missed the way the twisted arms shot upward in graceful arcs tipped with silver openings, like parted lips. The candelabra had been left behind in the city when Itte Binne was thrown out of her apartment.

At first it was possible to obtain Sabbath candles in the ghetto, but each month the candles grew darker, yellower, and smaller. They were made of a substance that had absolutely nothing in common with the white resplendence of authentic Sabbath candles. These pathetic shrunken substitutes even blushed to be seen in the hands of Jewish merchants, as if enduring the same hunger and humiliation as the ghetto Jews. And as the Sabbath candles shrank, so the Sabbath itself diminished. The Sabbath and the candles vanished together, eliminated from the bare tables of Jewish dwellings.

Now, Itte Binne is in line with a hundred other Jewish women in a large courtyard, holding her pot under her arm, waiting for soup.

The once prosperous woman is wrapped in a shawl, her head tilted to the side, staring aimlessly at the wall. In front of her is a gray-haired man, all huddled up, with a red scarf around his neck. This man's ears are large and stand away from a head overgrown with thick curly hair. His bony shoulders are slightly hunched, like those of her Saul, may he rest in peace. The patch on his hunched back hangs precariously by a few slack strands of yellow and green thread. Behind Itte Binne is a young girl with a yellow freckled face and a drooling open mouth showing widely spaced loosened yellow teeth.

The line stretches the entire length of the courtyard, then curls around toward an open window where two women are pouring gray soup from a cauldron into individual pots presented to them.

It is ten o'clock in the morning.

The last few weeks lunch has been portioned out very early. It is consumed quickly and then one goes around hungry the rest of the day. Since the soup kitchens have gone into operation, the streets fill up early in the morning with men running to be first in line, and women and children carrying pots. Now, their sunken faces showing the fearful inroads of vicious bitter hunger, they have formed a line. There are men with long beards who are wearing old wrinkled caps, worn-out Polish berets tossed carelessly on their heads, instead of traditional Jewish hats. The women's hollow cheeks resemble unleavened rolls, and are flecked with yellow spots left over from serious illnesses. Those in line shuffle forward one by one. The empty pots they hold in front of them look like the eager mouths of predatory animals. They sigh and moan hollowly from their caved-in chests. An unusual stink emanates from these people: from their clothes, from their hands, and even from their movements. Those who catch a whiff of that odor try to put some distance between themselves and the other people in the line. But wherever they go, the stench follows. They step out of line, but the stench clings to them like a garment. They move a few steps farther away before realizing that no matter what they do, they can't escape that stench. Perhaps that stench is a result of the human body, exposed to extreme hunger, consuming itself. From their limited

perspective these people cannot understand how quickly contin-
uous hunger breaks down the human body. The color of a
starved body is peculiar — the yellowish gray of sand, like the yel-
low-gray wall Itte Binne is staring at. Unseeing, her eyes are
glued to a piece of crumbled brick. When the people in the line
stop talking, they can stare aimlessly for hours at something that
is not even there: a scrap of cloud hanging from a shredded
rooftop; the fence across the way; a pebble; a grain of sand; a
strand of thread; or a solitary sliver of wood rolling in the sand at
their feet.

A loud grating sound is heard from behind the end of the line,
and before anyone knows what is happening, a wagon barges into
the sandy courtyard and stops not far from the line. A heavy sallow man and a boy leap down from the wagon, the boy dragging
a long unpolished board with him. On the roof of the wagon is a
four-cornered crate draped in black cloth. The inside of the
wagon is full. There is no room for any more corpses.

"Moishe Chaim, couldn't you find a better place to park your
wagon than in front of the soup kitchen, eh?" someone shouts
out the window of the kitchen to the two people who are at this
moment preoccupied with the board.

Moishe Chaim, the sallow, thick man from the wagon, moves
closer to the window.

"Who's that in the kitchen taking my name in vain, eh?"

"It's me, Shloime Zalman. I'm asking you, can't you find any
better place for your wagon than here, eh?"

The men shake hands through the open window. The man
inside has thick hairy hands with blue stiff veins. Moishe Chaim
has a round fat palm with short stumpy fingers.

"What're you cooking today, Shloime Zalman?"

"What should I be cooking? We're cooking rain water fla-
vored with well water" — the man inside shouts out the window,
and winking to the people standing and waiting in line, he whis-
pers something in Moishe Chaim's ear:

"Am I preparing merchandise for you, or what, Moishe
Chaim?"

The people in line look at the two men conversing. The insipid
expressions on their faces cloak a loathesome secret they keep

hidden from the world, as they would a sacred oath. A wet steam issues from the open window of the kitchen, settling on the black walls of the wagon. The people in line now hold the pots closer to their swollen bellies; they look at the wagon and then at the unpolished crate on the roof of the wagon. In a single stroke, the black wagon that has so abruptly planted itself right in front of their eyes has ruined their appetites. The people have forgotten their purpose in coming here; they can't remember why they are standing in the line, which has stopped moving. The shriveled heads atop withered necks are suddenly possessed by memories. Images of dead children, deceased relatives, and Jewish homes washed away in the deluge float before the inner eye. Only when the young boy from the wagon goes into the little office do the people rouse themselves from their stupor. They start speaking rapidly, in low tones. They speak about death, the particularly torturous painful death reserved for Jews. They say the dead are better off than the living, that it is a question of one more week, one more day. . . . Everybody standing here, they say, will eventually fall into Moishe Chaim's hands, and maybe into that very wagon, that very crate, to which their sad and mournful eyes are glued this very minute.

Shloime Zalman asks of Moishe Chaim:

"Would you be so kind as to move your buggy out of here, Moishe Chaim? I can't dole out lunch. . . . I can't get it over the . . ."

"Go on, go ahead, you jerk," Moishe Chaim adds with a nod, turning to Itte Binne, who by this time has reached the window; his glance passes from her to the group of people standing behind her, then back to her.

"Isn't that the way it is, Jewess?"—he says, addressing himself directly to Itte Binne. The woman lifts her face and looks straight into Moishe Chaim's eyes. The pot falls out of her hands and lands on the ground. Someone behind her bends down, picks up the pot, and places it back in her hands. At the same moment, a cry can be heard from inside the little office. And at that moment something snaps in Itte Binne's mind.

She apparently sees her husband, Saul, expiring in some corner of a strange house inhabited by unknown people. Next, she sees her eldest son imploring: "Mama, I can't take any more, I can't. . . ."

Then she sees Bracha, the bride. These were all events that had taken place the first winter in the ghetto. Present in all of Itte Binne's visions is the Jew, Moishe Chaim, with his stubby fat hands and soft yellow face.

By the time Moishe Chaim and the boy drag the board with the corpse onto the wagon, Itte Binne has already received her pot of soup. She holds the pot against her chest, not knowing what to do next. Her feet are rooted to the ground, and her eyes gaze aimlessly into thin air. As he turns, the horse pulling the death-cart pokes her in the shoulder with the shaft of the wagon. The wailing from the office follows the wagon. Standing in that sea of Jewish lamentation, Itte Binne has the feeling that she is the one they have just loaded onto the wagon.

She sits down on the pump, still holding her pot.

The line has thinned out. Itte Binne just sits there, the pot of cooked food at her side. Children from the courtyard gather around her. They look at her warily, and seeing that her eyes do not blink, they grow bolder and tighten the circle around her. One of them touches the pot, which is still warm. He lifts the lid: gray, turgid soup. His eyes start glittering. He sees that the old lady is not all there. One of the children tries taking the pot. Itte Binne does not resist. They run into a corner with the pot, but in their haste the pot slips out of their hands, and the soup is soon soaking into the sandy ground. The children pounce on the damp ground and, like little puppies, cup the wet sand into their palms and press it into their little mouths. They push, shove, and bite each other till nothing remains where the soup spilled but a jagged spot of gray earth from which it is no longer possible to lick a drop of fluid. . . . While the children wipe their mouths, sand gritting between their teeth, Itte Binne doesn't move. After a while, she stands up, removes the kerchief from her head, and spreads it on the ground in front of her. With empty fingers she scatters something on the cloth. The children run out of the courtyard in terror. Itte Binne continues scattering something from her empty hands, as if throwing feed to chickens. Then she claps her hands as one does when calling chicks. Her eyes roll heavenward and recede back into her head. Her empty pot lies upside down in the sand.

A round tin wagon, pulled by two men, rolls into the court-yard to collect the garbage. The men's ritual fringes hang out from under their tattered jackets. As they come closer they cast off the ropes they use to pull the cart and sit down on the pump next to Itte Binne. Before getting on with their work, they want to savor a morsel of bread. They pull out a few ragged pieces of white linen and try wrapping them around their hands. They always do this when they are about to touch a piece of bread. Noticing Itte Binne sitting on the pump, they call out to her:

"Would you be so kind as to wrap the linen around our hands?"

She has just finished chasing away the few fluttering chickens and has started to get to her feet. She takes the shreds of white linen from the two Jews and starts wrapping them around their hands. The Jews devoutly offer a silent blessing.

While the men are reciting their blessing over the bread, it seems to them that the woman beside them is also moving her shriveled lips. To tell the truth, Itte Binne is no longer with them. At the very moment she was bending over the men's wrapped hands, she was lighting her magnificent Sabbath candles in the tall dazzling silver candelabra.

On the tip of the pump post, a sunbeam that has managed to poke through a dying cloud frolics merrily.

Łódź Ghetto, 1941

Snow

Ice cold and razor sharp, the autumn wind had gathered bluish little mounds of snow, carried them wildly over rooftops and courtyards, then poured them with a thrashing howl into the cracks and crevices of walls and roofs. The whistling of the wind intensified the deep silence of a night brooding over the ghetto with distant twinkling stars. Somewhere on the northern plains beyond the wire, the same wind later burst into icy demonic laughter. Only a few cherry trees and some wild bushes remained in the sandy fields stretching from the cemetery on the northern side of the ghetto. By this time very few of the houses still there were inhabited. Beyond this wasteland lay the Brzezin Road, which wound its way to the Warsaw highway.

During the two years that the ghetto had been in existence, the cemetery had grown to a sizeable death-city. Thousands of little wooden boards set up as monuments covered the earth. In the summer they were completely submerged under tall weeds and wild roses; in the winter they were covered by a sheet of soft snow. Looking at the broad expanse of fields from a distance, one would never know that an entire city of dead Jews was at rest beneath the snow.

That year the winter was exceptionally severe. The silver-blue frost floated in thin cloudlets from the nearby fields, taking one's breath away and forcing the ghetto dwellers to remain in bed, wrapped up in their clothes. Many did not venture outdoors for weeks at a time. For days at a stretch the sun was frozen in its tracks and would hang mockingly in heaven. One evening, just before twilight, the snow shifted, driven by an icy wind; it came down all night, every now and then permitting a thin green stripe of frigid distant stars to slip through its windy arms.

As midnight drew near, German guards sat bundled up in their sentry boxes outside the wire fence, peering intently through the cut-out holes at the blinding snow dance in the ghetto. The wind, as it hurled itself at the wall around the cemetery, reinforced with barbed wire installations, played a stinging metallic melody. Hearing the suspicious sound, the German tore out of the guard house every now and then and uttered a shout into the night with a wild wolfish howl: "H-a-a-a-l-t!" At the same time he would draw his gun and wait. The echo of his shout reverberated across the dark silent fields and sank under the cemetery. The wires kept shivering in the cold light of the electric lamps. Not the shadow of a human being was to be seen. The German stood a while alongside the wires, gun drawn. The silence intensifies. He hears the whirling snow falling on the surrounding fields. Maybe it is only the snow-wind? And maybe, the German thinks, it is only the nightly rustling of Jewish ghosts, of the dead. But it is also possible that somewhere near the periphery, behind the cemetery, a Jew trying to get through has set the wires vibrating—that someone has stolen out of the ghetto on this snowy night and slipped into the nearby woods.

Sander did not worry about how the entire matter would turn out. For weeks one idea only had been gnawing away at his consciousness: escape! After the death of his mother and father, who had died of starvation, Sander was left with his eldest sister, Yetta. At first, he had kept the thought to himself, a thought casually uttered by his father as he was dying, something about escape. Already half a corpse, he had spoken of Jewish heroes, of Bar Kochba, of the Hasmoneans, of dying a martyr's death, of dedicating his soul to revenge. The few Jewish neighbors standing around his bed were weeping their age-old Jewish tears of passivity. At the sight of all that weeping, seeing the feeble impotence of his people, Sander himself broke into sobs.

After the mass killing, terror had settled into every Jewish dwelling, and the people simply awaited their fate. But Sander Stelmach, summoning what strength he had left, resolved to escape! He didn't reveal his secret to his sister immediately. But when he told her of his decision, she replied instantly that she was going with him. Rumors had been circulated by Jews caught out-

side the ghetto, and subsequently confined inside it, that somewhere not far from the Lenshitzer woods a group of escapees was
hiding out with decent peasants. Before the war Sander had
worked in his father's smithy, shoeing peasants' horses, so the
peasant language was not unfamiliar to him. At that time he had
filled out his tall, broad frame, with huge hands and broad shoulders. Now his skin hung on him in loose layers, like a garment
much too large for the wearer. His body seemed to wither and
shrink like a tree being stripped of its bark ring by ring. But
somewhere in a remote corner of his mind the flame of his
father's last words still flickered. In his heart, a secret and holy
thought continued to burn like a silver candelabra: Save yourself.
Escape!

Today, as evening fell, the two of them had edged toward the
cemetery. The little gate was still ajar, since it was customary to
continue burying the dead until late twilight. The grave diggers,
spades on their shoulders, had already retreated behind the wall.
The cemetery was empty. The whirling snow had settled on the
thorny bushes around the old Jewish tombstones. Sander and
Yetta were lying under a thin blanket of snow, next to the graves
of their father and mother. Yetta was near her mother's grave,
and behind her, across the path, Sander was lying at the grave of
his father. They had arranged earlier that this would be their last
stopping place before crossing the wire. From that spot to the
fence was a distance of only fifty to sixty steps.

In the few hours they had been lying on the frozen earth, the
snow had completely covered them and was now level with the
snow covering the graves.

Neither Sander nor Yetta was frightened by the darkness surrounding the cemetery. The more the wind whipped the mounds
of snow across the fields, the happier and more secure they began
to feel, as if a guarantee of life lay somewhere in the arms of the
winds blowing in from the distant steppes. Sander's breath melted the snow around his face. His bones had stiffened from lying
on the earth. He touched the mound of his father's grave with his
right arm, his mouth to the ground, murmuring something, his
eyes closed. He imagined that his father, a couple of yards
beneath him, was aware of everything happening, that he was

joyful, and that a smile was shaping itself on his dead face. But soon Sander started listening to the earthen mound over his father more carefully, straining his ears to the ground; the wind-driven snow passed over his head with a cold howl. The dead lay under the ground, sleeping their sleep. Sander silently begged his father's blessing. He told him that he and Yetta were setting out on a journey and that both of them would need abundant blessings on their dangerous excursion. "I am leaving this place, Father"—thus spoke a voice within him, wordlessly—"I am going to save my life and seek revenge, as was your holy wish. May your holy death, Father, and that of your dead neighbors, help me, protect me from danger. . . . I lie next to you and beg for our lives. I, Sander, beg you: Grant us your protection in this great danger, intercede with the Lord for our sake. . . ."

Meanwhile, Yetta was lying in silence next to her mother's grave, her head reclining on a mound of frozen sand. Her face was immersed in a veritable river. The flow of her tears was interminable and soaked inexorably into the sand of her mother's grave. She wanted to get out of here as soon as possible to be outside the ghetto. Lifting her head from under the snow, she saw the electric lamp swaying on the wires. In the whirlwind of snow, the light was a dark yellow, reddish near the outer rim. This was the most opportune time to slip under the wire fence. She wiped the snow off her face with her hand and transmitted a silent signal to Sander.

Lifting herself on both elbows and barely rising on one knee, Yetta dragged herself, completely covered with snow, lengthwise along the little path, directly to the wires. As she raised her head her eyes calculated the risk. The guards were nowhere to be seen. The snowstorm swept over the hilly cemetery as if it wanted to swallow the slightest sound completely and help the people get across the fence. An impenetrable darkness enveloped the surrounding fields, presaging the approach of dawn. It was essential to hurry. Yetta was the first to reach the fence, Sander was about ten paces behind her. She stopped for a moment, out of breath, stretched out in the snow. She searched carefully along the bottom level of wires, looking for the widest space through which to drag her body. She would have to to dig deeper under the snow to crawl snakelike under the wires. Yetta curled herself up and pressed herself to the earth as if she wanted to penetrate right into its snowy body. Her heart was thumping, it seemed to her, loud enough to be heard for miles around.

Yetta was on the other side of the wire. She was through. A deep, warm, human joy, along with a burning anxiety, poured out of her body. She sucked in the cold damp air; it was the air of freedom. As she went through, the bottom wire had not made even the slightest squeak. But stirred by the wind from the surrounding fields, the rusty barbed wires now sang out a melody of freedom. Yetta thought she would lie here a while, then roll her way down to the ditch, and then on to the forest, near the Brzezin Road. . . .

It was the hour before dawn, the moment when the darkness is deepest and most dense. Yetta was lying there covered with snow and night. Enveloped in freedom in an open world, she wallowed in the ditch as in a soft, warm pillow and waited for Sander.

The snow fell silently. The wind had subsided. Behind the fence, still in the cemetery, Sander was sliding on all fours, lengthwise along the narrow little path. The new blanket of snow covering the frozen earth had leveled the numberless death-mounds. He did not see Yetta any more. She was through, and now it was his turn to get to the other side. As he was propped on his belly the impatient fire that seemed to be consuming his flesh was extinguished by snow seeping into his sleeves in spite of his having tied them with laces at the wrists. That flame had strengthened him and kindled his heart like a prayer that brings one closer to God. He believed that he would overcome the danger. All the dead would protect his life, with the souls of his father and mother leading the way, holy and pure, and after them the rest of the dead, emerging from their white, snowy resting places.

The wind now started up on the other side of the fence. The snow frolicked above the wires. Just one more thrust forward and his head would be at the crossing point. It was a good thing that the wind was whistling now. And in that whistling of the wind, one could also hear the cry of a nocturnal bird. He trembled— and remained lying there a moment.

His body was already halfway across the fence when the

muted echo of an explosion sounded in the distance, and at the same time Sander felt a burning sliver streak across his forehead. His first thought was—I probably scratched my forehead on a wild thornbush. As he tried to move, a hot flush spread across his face. A thin stream with a sticky warmth flowed directly into his mouth. That thin stream started to warm his cheeks more and more and flowed down his throat. He tried moving his right foot—but he couldn't, as if some inner will of the cemetery refused to let him go, as though the dead were holding him back. He coiled his flattened body in order to tear himself out, but his body fell back, lame. It all took place so quickly that he could not figure out what had happened. Then the sliver of consciousness that still glowed in a remote corner of his mind understood, and Sander summoned all the strength in his limbs to push himself back into the cemetery, crawling backward a few steps.

He was lying at rest, his face splattered with blood. He still breathed fitfully in harmony with the snow and wind. But soon his breathing grew stiller and then stopped.

Meanwhile, the snow continued to fall without stop. A silence, which seemed to have lifted itself from under the snow, hung in the desecrated air. It was not long before the snow had completely covered his body and nothing could be seen but a flat field. Deep under the snow the dead slept their long sleep.

Finally, daylight arrived. On the eastern horizon, gray-white spots could been seen. The last snow clouds drifted away before the onslaught of the morning light, but among their folds, on the deep blue night-heaven, the last unextinguished stars continued to twinkle.

1942

Jews

Heavy rain drips sadly down the gray windowsills, and a thick mist hovers above the soft dark earth of the courtyard. Itshe Ber, leaning his wide face toward the window, presses his beard to the glass and looks down into the courtyard. It is the moment between afternoon and evening prayers. A reddish-black speck resembling clotted blood is a lingering reminder of the setting sun. For some time now, Itshe Ber has been standing at the window, staring at the roofs across the way that have just absorbed the sad beams of fading sunlight. Having just finished reciting afternoon prayers, Itshe Ber shuts his left eye while pressing his forehead to the pane. The cold soaking rain keeps pouring, as the Polish autumn smothers the ghetto in black clouds, patches of dark sky, and infinite grayness. Somewhere outside the ghetto, there must be naked trees, their dead-leaf gold scattered across the roads. But in the courtyard that is the object of Itshe Ber's gaze, the dreary Polish fall has arrived early without dead leaves and withered grass. In the ghetto there is only a wet autumn wind driving rain relentlessly into the windowpanes of wooden ghetto huts.

Sarah Leah stands near the oven in a dark corner of the room. One can hear the crackling of a meager fire coming from the oven. The evening meal is cooking—a dark, watery soup without potatoes, without any kind of grain, and without greens; it is an insipid brew of water and the rotted cabbage leaves left over from today's noonday meal. Itshe Ber's wife sighs incessantly. Hands folded on her bosom, she nods her head and sways. From the pot comes a brackish steam that makes one's eyes smart.

As Itshe Ber shuffles back into the room, Sarah Leah complains from the darkness, "This food—forgive me, sweet Lord, for speaking evil—but it's not even fit for animals."

Pretending not to have heard his wife's remark, Itshe Ber takes a seat and asks, "So, what do you think, Sarah Leah, are we going to have a bite to eat?"

Sarah Leah doesn't answer. She pulls a broad tablecloth out of a pile heaped on top of a bundle of bedding in a corner. The unfolded tablecloth spreads a whiteness through the room, a cool holiday whiteness, as when the moon sometimes suddenly appears above the rooftops. They had just moved into this apartment yesterday. They had set up the meager bedding they managed to bring with them, and were still trying to get themselves organized. At first, the small empty rooms had struck them as identical to all the other abandoned dwellings: little black holes. But the rooms have already started to feel homier, warmer, and now, with the dark rain pounding the courtyard, one might even say, cozier. Darkness has settled on the ghetto windows like an angry crow.

No sooner has he eaten his first spoonful of soup than Itshe Ber lowers his head and perks his ears. A heavy shuffling of feet can be heard from the stairs outside the flat. The dilapidated building, partly dismantled by its previous occupants, is empty, except for the two rooms that Itshe Ber and Sarah Leah have managed to salvage. The ground-floor apartments in the rear have been completely demolished. The gaping window frames have no panes. The doors have been torn from their hinges; the floorboards have been ripped out, exposing a deep cellar that fills the house with a moldy stench and ominous noises resembling the ghastly groans of the sick and dying. The interior walls have been ripped out or have collapsed. The stairs have been taken apart and the few boards remaining are unsteady, practically suspended in midair. The entire place resembles a poorhouse reeking of death and destruction. Not that this particular building is unique. All the wooden houses in the ghetto are in the same condition, taken apart by human beings who use the wood as fuel, trying to keep their sickly, swollen bodies warm. When Itshe Ber hears the sound of feet stomping outside the front door, he gets up uneasily and, grasping the tablecloth in his fist, calls out:

"Sarah Leah, who can be coming to visit us, huh? Things aren't the way they used to be. . . ."

Sarah Leah perks her ears:

"I won't let them cross the threshold, do you hear? I won't let them in, and that's the end of it."

"Eh, eh," Itshe Ber mutters. "First thing, you fly off the handle. Where are they supposed to go? Can they just wander around the streets on a night like this? Just take a look at what's going on outside."

"I don't care one bit. For all I care, it can rain and storm with thunder and lightning. . . . Let them go where they want, as long as it's not here. . . . I can't stand to look at them, at those disgusting faces."

"But even if they're a little peculiar Sarah, they're still Jews, . . . the children of Abraham, Isaac, and Jacob. . . ."

The old lady bursts out angrily:

"Is that what you think Jews are supposed to be like? Well, excuse me. . . . They don't understand a word of Yiddish. They don't look anything like Jews. I wouldn't be surprised if they wear little icons of Jesus on their hearts. . . . I'll be damned if they'd recognize a word of Torah. Now, I ask you, how can you call them Jews?"

"They're Jews, they're Jews," Itshe Ber retorts, trying to cool his wife's wrath. "If they weren't Jews, would they have sent them to live with us in the ghetto, from as far away as Berlin and Hamburg, Prague and Vienna?"

That instant the door opens, and four or five shades can be seen standing in the darkened threshold. The people are wrapped in furs and raincoats. They are cloaked in hoods of a kind not ordinarily worn by Jews and carry little suitcases, expensive valises completely soaked by the rain. Their faces are barely visible under the partly opened hoods. In the darkness it is difficult to tell the women from the men. They are all wearing pants and sturdy sport shoes. One of them, stepping out of the darkness, walks into the room and takes off his little narrow hat with a feather tucked into the hatband; he looks like an alpine hunter just come down from the mountain. He is wearing high laced boots and has leather bags hanging from both shoulders; on his back he carries a rucksack. This person clears his throat twice, wipes the moisture from his smooth-shaved head, and going directly up to Itshe Ber, starts speaking in a peculiar drawl that definitely is not Yiddish:

"*Guten A-a-a-a-vent, Meine Herrschaften.*" ("Good evening, sir and madam.")

"Praise the Lord, welcome the honored guests," Sarah Leah shouts, clapping her hands and screwing up her face as if she were about to start crying. "Just take a look at your pious Jews."

She turns her back to the strangers and continues to mutter in a corner of the room near the stove:

"Has anyone ever been afflicted with such a visitation? We don't have enough troubles—all I need is these foreign gentry on my back."

While the old lady putters around her kitchen, Itshe Ber, after examining some kind of document the stranger has shown him, ushers the people into the second room, a dark and dank little hole that is completely empty. The people drag all their suitcases and bundles into the room, even hatboxes containing old hats and other headgear.

A flash of light suddenly illuminates the rafters overhead. They have lit a candle in the room, set it on one of the trunks, and have sat down on the cold floor.

In the other room, Sarah Leah has not stopped her verbal assault on Itshe Ber:

"As I live, I wouldn't have let that bunch cross the threshold. . . . You call them Jews? Those are heathen, not Jews. Did you get a look at their clothes? Is that how people dress when they're going to prison? They're dolled up as if they were going to a masquerade ball. . . . O Lord, may your Jewish folk be damned! . . . They should be sitting in sackcloth and ashes, mourning, not meandering from house to house."

Itshe Ber does not try to silence his wife, because he knows from experience that she will soon quiet down. It would be worth his life to utter a syllable; one peep out of him would provoke a verbal onslaught like a raging river at flood tide breaking through a dam; she would drown him in a torrent of words. So he just turns his face to the wall, crawls into a corner, and prepares for evening prayer.

In the small room, the strangers sit on their leather suitcases and bags without uttering a word. It is as if they have all fallen instantaneously into a deep sleep. The door is open a crack, and Sarah Leah turns from her cooking every few minutes to peek through a crevice, curious to see what the "clowns" are up to in there. All she sees are people sitting on their suitcases, small snow-white napkins tied under their necks, like bibs, eating crumbs of dry stale cake they pluck out of one hand with the other.

By now, Itshe Ber has started his evening prayers. He starts ever so quietly, barely moving his lips. But soon he opens his hands, spreads them wide, and starts clapping them like a huge bird flapping its wings, as if he were literally soaring on the wings of prayer, as if he wants to tear himself away from this spot, fly away from the dark corner, and remove himself to some secluded, green valley, where he can pray with unrestrained passion. His words are burning coals that ignite the surrounding void. At first, the words set fire to his clothes, then to the air around him, and finally, the floor starts to go up in smoke. He tosses to and fro like a tree rocked by thunder and struck by lightning. He raises his hands above his head, and spreads his fingers as if he imagines, and even fully believes, that his feet are no longer touching the wooden floor. With his fists folded on his breast, Itshe Ber sighs and groans, tears pieces of flesh out of his body, and pounds his temples.

His wife tends to her cooking; she can't figure out what's happening to him. A hot wind is blowing from the corner where Itshe Ber is praying. It has been a very long time since she has heard him pray with such passion. It is no longer Itshe Ber standing in that corner, but a fiery angel, shouting and lamenting. Now, she even hears weeping coming from the corner, and that weeping strikes terror into her heart. Sarah Leah no longer recognizes her Itshe Ber. It is as if a consuming angel has taken his place in that darkness, and it is that angel who is praying and supplicating for the fate of all the Jews in the whole world.

While Itshe Ber is saying his evening prayers, something is going on in the other room, where the strangers have made themselves at home. Itshe Ber falls silent and listens in wonder. Is he really hearing what he thinks he hears? At first, it seems to him that what he hears is coming from inside himself, from somewhere in his own heart. And who can say? Maybe his own prayer is suspended in the void, and this strange melody, resembling the song of a flock of summer birds, is an echo wafted into the ghetto on a silken zephyr, reverberating in the air and harmonizing with a myriad of silver bells.

Through the open door, a subdued song, sung to a melody bearing no resemblance whatever to the Jewish liturgy, can be heard coming from the adjacent room. The delicate ecclesiastical melody wafted from the next room is rich with a strange scent of incense and paganism. A female voice breaks through the choral chant, and this solo voice sustains the melody while the others merely support the soloist with a deep, harmonious accompaniment. One might think that the melodies flooding in from the next room are organ notes interweaving with the passionate words of prayer being uttered in an exotic tongue.

This is more than Sarah Leah can bear. Absolutely inflamed with rage, she opens the door. Itshe Ber stands behind her, confused, peering into the inner depths of the room. In the darkened chamber the strangers are standing rigidly upright, with their hands clutched to their breasts, their heads hung down, and their eyes shut. They continue singing that same distant, foreign song. The valises they have brought with them are strewn across the floor, and the flickering candle, dripping wax on a trunk, sputters. The singing ceases, and the whole room is filled with the cool hushed darkness of a cathredal. The now silent strangers, wrapped in a fog of darkness, stand frozen and petrified like a row of monks.

Sarah Leah can't contain herself any longer. Unable to restrain the powerful wrath welling up within her, she waves her hand angrily and cries out:

"A black pestilence on them! Out of my place with your heathen chanting! Has anyone ever seen such a plague? They've gone and turned a Jewish home into a sinkhole of impurity. May they be cast into outer darkness. . . ."

The strangers, who do not understand a word of Yiddish, just stand there motionless, like statues frozen in prayer.

"Sha-a-a-ah—There's no need to be so angry, Sarah Leah,"

Itshe Ber ventures from behind his wife. "Sha-a-a-ah, have a little respect for Jews. . . . Can't you see that Jews are praying?"

Meanwhile, the people inside open their eyes and smilingly sit down on the floor. They look as if they've just wakened from a deep sleep. Itshe Ber goes into the room and begins discussing something with the one who looks like an Alpine hunter. Itshe Ber is trying to speak pidgin German, but the German doesn't understand a word. He just extends a skinny hand to Itshe Ber, smiling broadly and showing his cold, white teeth. Itshe Ber winks to Sarah Leah, who is still standing in the doorway, angry as ever, and calls out in a voice that sounds as if he were still praying:

"Isn't it about time you gave them something warm to eat, Sarahle? Don't you see? These Jews are soaking wet from the rain. . . . How long do they have to wait? How long?"

In a short while, Sarah Leah brings small cups of warm soup into the room on a tray she had snatched from its hiding place just as they were leaving the city apartment from which they were being expelled. For a moment, she stands motionless in the middle of the room. The tray rests a bit unsteadily on her broad work-hardened hands, as warm steam curls around her arms. For a long time, not one of the strangers reaches out for the soup. Their hands are occupied with the little silk handkerchiefs with which they are wiping the tears from their eyes. From under the hankies flows a torrent of sweet gentle words:

"*L-i-e-ber bruder, L-i-e-ber shvester . . . Danke, danke. Wir zind doch alle Ju-den, Ju-den, Ju-den.*" (D-e-a-r brother, d-e-a-r sister . . . Thank you, thank you. We are, after all, all Jews, Jews, Jews.)

Their embarrassed words drop to the floor and are shattered into tiny splinters of tinkling glass.

Łódź Ghetto, 1942

✿

The Sorcerer

The apartment in which Heinz Friedrich Levi of the third Berlin transport lived was a dark alcove like a monk's cell, with a slanted gothic window high on the wall.

To the other Jews who lived in that little courtyard, Heinz Friedrich Levi was a mystery. He was never seen leaving the courtyard on his way to some kind of work; he was never seen going down to the well to wash a bowl; and no one had ever seen him come down to the courtyard in the evening to enjoy some fresh air. People used to say that the German would leave his attic room only with the rising of the moon, and then you would see him going somewhere with a black fur piece under his arm, wrapped up like a black shroud, as though he were carrying a dead child under his arm.

It often happened that the Jews in the courtyard where Heinz Friedrich lived would suddenly stop short in the middle of the courtyard and stare up at his tilted window with puzzled looks on their faces. The violin music that wafted down from his attic room into the courtyard served as a bittersweet reminder to the Jews who lived there of days gone by, of weddings graced with the joyful playing of Klezmer musicians. Most often this happened on nights when the courtyard lay bathed in the cool silver of a full moon that had blundered into the courtyard from an open and unrestricted world.

The German's fiddling kept everyone awake. The sad melodies coming from that narrow window bathed in green moonlight were enough to break your heart. But more than once, some Jewish woman would furiously open a window and shout:

"Why doesn't that vile sorcerer let anyone sleep? May he go to the Devil up there in his attic!"

Heinz Friedrich Levi terrified people with his black fur bundle and his nocturnal fiddling. During the day he stayed in the attic, never opening his window, so the Jews started saying that the German must be some kind of outlandish creature, a sorcerer. . . .

One day Heinz Friedrich Levi woke up on his trundlebed with a splitting headache. All night he had been tormented by bizarre, unearthly dreams: one minute he would see himself strolling on the wide boulevards of Berlin, then all at once the streets would shrink, grow narrow, and what had but a moment ago been a broad boulevard became a narrow wagon. Lying in the dark wagon, he watched trees, houses, and people flash by through a barred window. . . . The next instant he would see himself near a large water mill, its huge wheels turning. With each turn smiling children, with blooming ruddy cheeks, would fall off the wheels. They sat on the ground, braiding wreathes, which they threw into the flowing water, where the wreaths appeared to swim upstream toward the mill.

Heinz Friedrich Levi lowered his feet to touch the floor, then pushed a finger into the flesh of his belly, testing to see how swollen his body was. Then he rubbed his eyes and strolled over to the bucket of water in the corner.

He abruptly reminded himself of something, and a ray of light lit up his swollen face, like sun cavorting on flowing water.

On his way to the bucket of water, the German recalled that a wedding was supposed to take place in the next courtyard. He had been invited because the people there knew he had a fiddle. At a Jewish wedding there must be music, even in the ghetto. He had remembered that the wedding was to take place today. He polished his wooden shoes with a wet piece of cloth and put on his last silk shirt from Berlin. But he could not get his soft blue eyes to take on a festive expression. They were islands of gloom embedded in watery cushions, and reflected in them was a terrified expression one might find in the eyes of a sick dog.

As evening approached, the door opened and two Jews entered.

"Well, Mister, we've come to escort you to the wedding, but bring your fiddle with you, do you hear?"

"Good, good—very nice, very nice," smiled the forlorn German, at the same time pulling the black fur from under the trundle bed.

In a sweaty, cramped, dark room, Jews were conducting a wedding. There were about about twenty guests from the surrounding courtyards. A sour aroma of reheated flat potato rolls permeated the room. Sad women who kept pinching their drawn cheeks were sitting around on dark, wet chairs:

"Damn us, chosen ones," one of the women called out. "This ain't what a Jewish wedding's supposed to look like."

Another woman chimed in: "Not a scrap of fish . . . not a morsel of bread! Ain't it a shame?"

"Sin not in your speech, chattering women," interrupted a guest with a pointed little chin out of which grew a few strands of blond hair. "May there be enough flat potato rolls to satisfy everyone. . . . This is actually honey cake, not potato rolls at all."

Next to the window, enveloped in a thick fog, as if under a veil, sat the bride and groom, two emaciated children. The parents were rushing the wedding through because they were afraid the ghetto would soon be liquidated. At least let the children be joined in wedlock. In this dark room reeking to the rafters with soursmelling steam, the young newlyweds shared a deep secret of faroff joy. On her exposed yellow neck, the bride wore a white scarf, its tassels cascading down her young shoulder like scattered rays. Her fingers toyed nervously with the tassels. The two of them sat there, famished, looking into each other's eyes. The groom had healthy teeth that would have done justice to a loaf of coarse peasant bread. But this was a wedding without bread—just a bit of dark soup, bitter coffee, and reheated potato rolls.

As the wedding feast got under way, the Jew from Germany was asked to take out his fiddle.

"Play something, Mister German," urged a chorus of voices from all corners of the room. "After all, this is a Jewish wedding."

"Play, play, Mister German, play some kind of a joyful song, some jolly melody."

Heinz Friedrich Levi did not need much urging. He removed the fiddle from the dark fur wrapping, adjusted his chin, and, with glazed eyes, began to fiddle.

He played with his eyes closed, the cushions of water swishing around them. He propelled the bow with his swollen hand, while the fingers on the fingerboard were so swollen they covered the entire neck of the violin. A deep cool melody, some sort of liturgy, settled on everyone's heart. The exhausted Jews drank in the melody with the warm steam as if it were a glass of cool mountain water. The newlyweds sat very close to each other, their hands entwined in a warm embrace under the tablecloth. The German played on in this manner, then abruptly opened his eyes. The water-cushions swished around, as if they had just been roused from a tortured sleep, and fixed their gaze on the audience.

The fiddler sat down, wiping the sweat from his forehead. After a moment's silence he called out to the nearby Jews:

"Doth thou know who that was? That, my good sirs, was Schubert. . . Schubert. . . ."

"Let me be, and save me from such scraping," interrupted a young man with a pair of dull eyes. "We'd much rather hear a jolly song, a happy Jewish tune. . . ." And in the blink of an eye the young man grabbed the fiddle out of the German's hand.

Pale and frightened, Heinz Friedrich Levi collapsed into a chair, fluttering his eyelashes, while the young man with the dull eyes played a merry tune. In an instant, the German dropped his head into his hands; the people sitting next to him moved away and shouted:

"Just take a look. . . . The German, the sorcerer, is actually crying."

The German did not move from the spot. He kept his head down and wiped his eyes with his sleeve.

He stood up, his chin trembling—and with a tremulous voice that frightened the celebrants, cried out:

"But my dear people, that was Schubert, Franz Schubert! . . ."

"Give him back his fiddle, and let the German go. . . . He seems to be a bit loony. . . ." A woman with a pockmarked face, overwhelmed by a sudden rush of pity for the German, took the fiddle away from the young man, and putting it under the German's arm, led him to the door.

"Be so good as to leave, Mister German, in health and in peace, and may the Lord grant that we may someday share in your own joyful occasion."

In the low-ceilinged alcove that resembled a monk's cell, Heinz Friedrich Levi, upon coming home from the wedding, put the fur piece back in its place beside the trundle bed, and, heaving a sigh of pain, threw off his wooden shoes. He tried probing his thick flesh again, and this time his finger remained stuck in it. He let himself down onto the edge of the trundle bed and with glazed eyes stared at the open fiddle cover. He gazed and gazed—and the moonbeams flowed into the room with an eerie silence. He got up from the trundle bed. The fiddle peeped out of the fur in which it was wrapped. Then, still in his clothes, he lay down on the bed again and closed his eyes. Before long, he fell asleep.

As he slept, the rays of the moon played in the room. Streaks of green light slid across the walls and over the face of the sleeper. In the enchanted moonlight, mice started crawling out of the woodwork—hungry, black, and noisy. The mice ran along the walls, crawled over the fur cover, and entangled their feet in the strings of the fiddle. As they ran along the strings, the fiddle would every now and then weep in a high-pitched voice. Once again the German dreamed a strange unearthly dream. He enters a garden where someone is leading him by the hand. He lifts his eyes and is astonished: it is none other than Schubert, Franz Schubert himself! They walk along under shady trees, then come to a halt. He stretches out his hand to grab a branch, and his arm is instantly transformed into a violin. As the wind wafts across its strings, it cries out in a strange voice, the voice of a weeping child.

The light of the moon now disappears in the radiance of the morning stars. A gray light hangs loosely on the trundle bed, as if a sheet has been thrown over it. Heinz Friedrich Levi is snoring heavily. The mice look out of their holes suspiciously. The violin strings continue to vibrate with a spectral transparency under the feet of the angry mice.

Łódź Ghetto, 1943

Survived

Hersh Leib, a man in his sixties, is lying on the cast iron bed while his wife, Tzippe, fusses around the room. She is short by nature and lately has shrunk still further. As a result of prolonged hunger, her green eyes are ringed by black and blue circles right to her nose. She is bent over a bowl, rubbing something with a brush. Every few seconds she groans, turns her head to the bed where Hersh Leib is lying sick and miserable, and hisses through her clenched teeth:

"It'll do. No delicacy will come out of this, no matter what . . ."

Having had her laugh, the old lady takes the "delicacy" of washed potato peels out of the bowl with both hands and wrings them one more time with her skinny fingers. A black slime with a sourish stink slithers through her hands. A nauseating rottenness, like the stench of a corpse that has been lying too long unburied, permeates the room.

Day is fading into evening. Ghetto nights are different from those outside. Like black birds carrying terrifying messages under their wings, ghetto nights swoop down suddenly on the wooden rooftops and hover outside the windows. You don't even notice the sun going down or the sky gradually extinguishing itself. Day vanishes behind the wire fences as chaotic raging night comes stalking into the ghetto in its angel-of-death cloak. Then the ghetto area—the ground, the streets, the dilapidated houses—becomes a solid block of darkness.

Night is already settling into the corner where Hersh Leib is lying.

In the darkness he can be heard gasping for breath.

"Tzippe, it's wasted ef . . . It's no use . . . I'm done for, any-way."

To his, "I'm done for anyway," she does not respond. His

words chill her like the coolness of embalming fluid, like the rustle of white cotton shirts being torn into shrouds.

Meanwhile, Tzippe has put the pot with the potato peels in the oven. The dry wood from the hacked-up bureau flares as though it has been soaked in benzene. The scraps of wood going up in smoke are the last remnants of the Sabbath bureau. When Tzippe had chopped it up for kindle wood, her heart had been overwhelmed with sadness. How could she destroy that little cabinet with its narrow carved doors, warped from many years of use? Time and again, those doors had been opened to yield their treasure, the two candelabras that would illuminate the Sabbath. Now the two brass candelabras have been tossed into some remote corner where they reside with an odd assortment of rubbish, while Tzippe uses the remnants of the Sabbath bureau to cook a few potato peels. In days gone by she would have let her hands be lopped off before using that bureau for kindle wood. But today—consumed by agony—what does it matter? She is no more than a shadow of what she used to be before both children had died. And who but Tzippe, crawling around on all fours in the ghetto garbage dumps to find a few rotten potato peels for Hersh Leib, who but Tzippe carries the entire yoke on her back? With her withered yellow hand she scratches around in the stench of the garbage dumps. Scavenging the garbage with Tzippe are the fat repulsive crows that are everywhere in the ghetto. Their angry, raucous crowing fills the ghetto streets. They soar over the rooftops in flocks, seldom alighting on the other side of the wires. These crows, attracted here from the empty fields nearby, are the sadness-and-death birds of the Jewish ghetto.

Since Tzippe first noticed the swelling on Hersh Leib's body, she has had no rest. The secret of the swollen mounds on his body is all too familiar to her. Both her children had perished of water around the heart. Now she can see it all happening again. But Hersh Leib may hold out for a long time before "the waters compass him about even to his soul." Tzippe is well informed about such matters: she has seen feet so swollen you couldn't tell where the foot ended and the ankle began. The flesh takes on a shiny whiteness, as if the skin were smeared with oil. The swelling then starts creeping up the calves to the knee, then the thigh, and then to the lowest rim of the belly, and by the time it gets to the navel the job is half done. In Hersh Leib's case the whiteness is barely beyond the calves, which are puffy, soft, and yellow. If you poke your finger into the skin, a deep hole remains. The flesh is watery and flabby. And the peels that Tzippe is cooking for him are pure water. How long, alas, can he survive on such nourishment?

Hersh Leib himself has already accepted the inevitable: since a whole people is going down the drain, he thinks, why should he, Hersh Leib, hold out? Why should he alone survive out of so many? It's all over. He lived, he died. But he can't help being angry at the casual way that corpses are treated here. It seems as if they just grab them quickly, toss them up onto the wagon with other corpses, women and children, the naked and the swollen. The dead seem to catapult themselves, with a hearty "Let's go!" onto the wagon that traverses the ghetto. Without shrouds, without Jewishness, they become no different than dogs flung into the earth. That thought really bothers Hersh Leib. He can't fathom such disorder. He would very much like to die as a Jew dies, the way his father and grandfather did: with candles near his head, with Jewish ritual, with purification and shrouds. . . .

And why die this very moment, when people are saying that salvation is near at hand? Rumor has it that the Germans are already running in panic on the other side of the Vistula, and if the rumors happen to be true, what is the point of a human being just going and dying? No, it's impossible. In what did he sin so egregiously that he should give up the ghost just as the ordeal is about to end? A prayer flows to his lips: "Oh God, give me the strength to hold out, give me the tenacity to keep on going. Don't hurl me back from the shore just when it is in sight. . . . Oh Lord, here I am drowning in the ocean; I stretch my hand out to You. . . . Don't repudiate me. Lead me safely to the shore. . . ."

And Hersh Leib, curled up on his bed in the darkness, presses his emaciated watery hands together, places them on his heart, and utters a prayer. He prays as he used to during the years of Jewishness, when he used to stand in the synagogue before the closed Holy Ark and sob before the Lord of the Universe. And now it is no longer his heart he squeezes with his hands, but the soft smooth silken curtain of the Holy Ark. His face glows with the tears running down his beard, and he conceals his head in the folds of curtain. His lips burn feverishly. New strength surges into his veins, and he feels certain his tears have been accepted. He feels as if a burden has been lifted from him, and within him his swollen heart, engulfed in fluid, sings a song of joy and salvation. He is strolling casually among tables covered with white tablecloths. Hundreds of black-bearded Jews are swaying in prayer and rejoicing. Sparkling decanters of wine with swanlike necks decorate the white tables. Jews are clapping their hands in joy and prancing across the floor. Only the beloved of the Lord have survived, have swum across the wide ocean of Jewish troubles, and he, Hersh Leib, is actually among them. . . . But where is Tzippe? A tall womanly shape, clothed in a silk dress, her hands laid upon her breast, as is her habit, steps out of a circle of Jews and comes straight up to him. Her glowing eyes are radiant with joy. The two of them embrace and start to dance automatically. Actually, they are too old to be dancing, but if they have lived to see this day, why not dance, especially since everyone else is dancing. The courtyard, the street, the surrounding houses: a city full of Jews has gathered and is dancing. The floors creak beneath pounding feet; long coats and traditional jackets swirl in the air. Even the musicians don't lag behind: fiddles, drums, and clarinets. A flute can be heard weeping sweetly, like a canary; two fiddles begin their message on a high note and say to the world: "Tri-ri-ri, at the appointed hour, survived, at the appointed hour, at the appointed hour! . . . tri-ri-ri."

Tzippe approaches the bed with the scraps of cooked peels. She pulls at his hands, still clasped on his heart. They fall away like dried-up twigs. His eyes are stuck open in the darkness.

His lips, now ice cold, are mumbling something silently to themselves. Tzippe bends over him.

"Survived, survived."

The words carry to her ears like a chill wind.

She throws herself on the bed with a scream:

"Ge-va-a-a-ald, Hersh Leib, how can you leave me behind?"

The scream hovers in the room for a long time, suspended in

the darkness like the sharp edge of a slaughterer's knife slicing
into a human throat.

Łódź Ghetto, 1943

✿

Bread

The little room where Mama Glikke has installed herself and her household goods, along with Shimmele and their two children, is nestled in the porch of the little house, its narrow little window looking down wistfully at the small street beyond the confines of the ghetto. Outside the ghetto, the little street runs like a narrow tunnel alongside the recently installed wire fences. The hovel itself—a wooden structure crumbling with age, sagging with the rains and snows of many generations—bows its roof ever closer to the top of the fence, like one who laments: "Oh—oh, what I have lived to see . . . Oh my, such a fate . . ." None of the roofs of the neighboring stone houses has taken up the rain-song of the autumn night, the joyful caresses of the glittering snow—and the luminous journeys of silvery moons—as has the crumbling roof on the old collapsing hovel.

From the narrow little window, "they" can always be seen below. For days now, and months, the black, shiny military boots have been pacing the bridge, back and forth, day and night, without stop. The German pacing here with his gun keeps on looking at the warped little house and at the tilted roof. The people inside the house do not come close to the little window, which is never opened more than just a crack, because when the German below sees an open window, or the shadow of a head—he shoots at it. As a matter of fact, at this moment the little window in Glikke's house is just the slightest bit ajar. It is a hot July day, and a dry, hot wind wafts through the narrow opening.

The room itself is white, calcined, with a wooden pole that descends straight down to the stove. The paint is peeling off the walls, littering the ragged floor, which here and there is missing a few boards. The Gentile who lived in the apartment before them and left before the Jews had been herded into the ghetto, took some of the floor with him when he departed, and took sections of the stove, too. When they moved in, Mama Glikke quickly set up a second stove, which now stands propped up on some red bricks. Billows of smoke rise from the improvised stove every time Mama decides to cook a hot meal. Not a stick of furniture, no closet, no beds. When the family had fled here, Mama Glikke had even brought a decent cabinet with her from the old place in the city. Back there, at home, a pair of silver Sabbath candelabras used to stand in the cabinet, behind glass doors. But, as it happened, the cabinet fell apart on the journey, as they were being hustled into the ghetto, and now the two Sabbath candelabras are lying on the floor in a corner near the window, in a pile of junk, among empty pots and torn clothes.

Set in one wall of the room is a little wooden door, and beyond the door, a tiny chamber, dark and narrow, where Mama has stored a bit of firewood and also the sides of the decrepit cabinet. A dark gloom pervades that tiny chamber, which seems stuck in perpetual twilight; behind the slanted studs old green spiders are spinning their webs. The Gentile who used to live here kept pigeons in the tiny chamber. A triangular opening had been cut in the wall facing the street, and through this opening the Gentile's doves would fly in and out. You can still find little grains of oats in the soil of the black earthen floor. The door to the little chamber is always closed, and Mama has forbidden the children, who are constantly digging holes in the earthen floor, from entering the room. It sometimes happens that a pigeon will fly up to the triangular opening and alight on the edge of a board. She's happened to find her way here because of a familiar wind or cloud, and she can't break her attachment to her old home. She pokes her head into the dark empty chamber and stands there trembling, frightened, her little red feet perched on the board's edge, looking around with surprised, innocent eyes. The pigeon soon flies away, beating her wings outside the window as if to say farewell: "Stay healthy! Who knows if we will see each other again?"

The mother and the father follow the same routine every day. At the crack of dawn, as soon as the sun appears on the eastern rim of the ghetto, Mama Glikke grabs two huge pots and takes up her post somewhere in a courtyard behind a fence. Mama stands there for hours, sometimes till late at night. There is a kitchen in the ghetto where they cook dinners for many people. The boys who carry water from the pump to the kitchen sense the desperate eyes of Mama Glikke staring through a crack in the fence. After the soup has been portioned out, the boys take the pots from her and ladle out a bit of turbid, diluted liquid. Though hunger gnaws at Mama's bowels, as if someone were tearing her flesh with a pair of pliers, and although she has been standing at the fence staring through the crack all day, still Mama does not taste a drop of the soup until she has returned to the little room. With two pots tucked under her shawl she runs across the ghetto like an athlete. She is terrified that, God forbid, she may spill a drop of soup, a spoonful of the holy fluid. She runs, and the two corners of her scarf flutter behind her like the wings of a large, frightened bird.

The labors of the father, Shimmele, are quite another matter. Sickly, with a chronic phlegmy cough and runny eyes overflowing with tears, the father sits all day in the room with the children, wrapped in his *tallis* and *tefillin*. He starts his prayers as soon as Glikke leaves, and does not take off the *tefillin* till just before evening. The children are afraid of the father. The last few days he has done nothing but stand near the wall for hours on end, wrapped in *tallis* and *tefillin*, not moving an inch. They imagine that father has been dead for some time, that out of the blue he has decided to give up his soul, that he is standing there with his face to the wall, stony, frosty, a dead man. And when he suddenly turns from the wall and gazes into the room after many hours of stony silence—the children see that their father's face is white as snow, his eyes soaked in tears. He sits down in the remotest corner of the room, covered with *tallis* and *tefillin*, and waits for the mother to walk through the door. And at his feet lie Avremele and Perele, terrified and lost.

Since they started rationing bread in the ghetto, hunger has haunted the room. At first, everyone shared: mother, father, and children. When they picked up their ration of bread and laid it on the table, it would lie there for a long time till the fastidious and fluttering mother took the knife, said a blessing, and tremblingly sliced the bread. Father and the children would gather around her, and after everyone had received a portion large enough to satisfy the initial pangs of hunger, mother would wrap the bread in a white cloth and stash it away so that no one would be able to find it. The bread would have to last for a long, long time. As if out of spite, when bread entered the room, hunger grew apace, tearing at the guts like a perverse imp. In dreams, fresh round loaves would swim into view and bring satisfaction. They knew that somewhere in the room a radiant treasure lay hidden. Oh, God, if only it were possible to cut slice after slice from the loaf and not be terrified by the knowledge that with every slice the loaf gets smaller and smaller. If only they could sit down and eat to their hearts' content. But that could only be a dream. In the meantime they cursed every bit of bread that touched the palate. The bread did not satisfy. With each bite, hunger's pangs sharpened. They examined each crumb of bread lying in their hands as if it were a diamond. Before putting it to the tongue they feasted their eyes on it, deriving bitter joy from the sight of the Lord's bounty.

Once there was a stroke of misfortune.

The day it happened, Mother couldn't stop cursing this wretched life. Something occurred that almost caused Father to hang himself out of pure shame. After that misfortune he spent whole days just lying on the floor, moaning. Who could have predicted such a thing? Mother just kept repeating: "Now there is nothing lower for him to stoop to, oh Master of the Universe, except to cut a chunk of flesh out of the children and cook it."

They did not know how it came to pass, and even the father himself did not know how things had come to such misfortune and disgrace. Shimmele couldn't fathom what force had urged him to do such a thing. He just did not know.

At that moment a tornado had raged in his heart. It could not have been his very own hands that in the darkness of the chamber stuffed the children's bread into his own mouth. No . . . no. That hadn't been the father anymore. It wasn't Shimmele, but some kind of enchanted shadow that had separated itself from him, that had issued from his hands and feet, some kind of accursed dybbuk who used the father's hands and fingers to tear at the dark, chestnut-flour loaf and salivate over it dozens of times. Wet, half-chewed chunks fell from his stuffed mouth and lay in his palms.

From there they were popped right back into the mouth that had spit them out in unnecessary haste. Afterwards, he had just stood there, benighted and petrified, his head buried in his hands.

The day the father ate the children's bread, Mama Glikke came home late. She found both children lying in a corner, famished. When she noticed that a quarter of a loaf was missing, she raised a racket, and it was only then that Shimmele crawled out of the little chamber. When she read the truth in his downcast eyes, she squawked like a slaughtered chicken:

"A father, eh? A fa-ther, is it? *Murderer!*"

And from that moment on the mother walked around worried and anxious, until she found a solution: she sewed two little sacks out of shirts and stuffed the sliced portions of bread into the sacks; in that manner she traversed the streets, the sacks slung over her heart.

The mother has nicknamed Avremele, Umele. He is slight in stature, with a thin, narrow little head and protruding ears, an exact replica of his father. His eyes, too, have a moistness about them, and if you were to look closely, knowing his elderly father, you would see from Umele's pinched expression and pointed chin that he will turn out exactly like the old man. Though Umele has not yet reached his twelfth birthday there is already fixed in his countenance a trace of his father's agedness and brokenness. Like the old man, he always keeps his hand on his bowed forehead, thinking of something. A restless shadow hovers over his pale, transparent cheeks. The few ghetto months have completely transformed the children. They are not children anymore, but a pair of old people, with the ravages of the last few years showing on their faces.

Umele is sitting on the floor, and next to him, at his side, his little sister, Perele. Perele has a slight limp; her thin, sandy-colored hair cascades down her narrow shoulders. They are both sitting in the corner near the Sabbath candelabras, gazing across at the opposite corner, where the father is busy with something or other. The mother left the room very early in the morning, taking the little sacks of bread with her, and now they are hoping that the father will leave the room soon, so that they can go back into the little chamber.

But it is a long, long time before the father leaves. He just keeps on looking at an open book. Since that day when the great disgrace occurred he has not been able to look the children straight in the eye. Buried in the pages of his book, he seeks something there with his tiny pinpoint eyes, and every now and then gives vent to the accumulated air in his lungs with a great, deep sigh and remains lying with his face buried in the book as if his throat has been cut. He doesn't move for a long time, dozes off, then wakes up abruptly when he hears the crash of the book as it falls out of his hands onto the floor.

Now the children watch as the father picks up the book, rummages around in his pocket looking for his key, and lets himself out the door.

When the two of them, Umele and Perele, see that they have been left alone, their eyes light up with glee. Umele runs quickly to the door of the little chamber and pulls out the nail that keeps the door fastened. The two of them run into the chamber, but as she is running Perele trips on the threshold. She gets up and chases after Umele, her foot dragging. By this time, Umele is already standing in the darkness of the chamber, near the wall that faces out onto the street. Umele had found a crevice in the wall. There are, in fact, two crevices, one a slight distance from the other. Umele takes up his vigil at one of these crevices, and stands there, watching.

Down below, on the other side of the street, across from the wires, there is a little store and the display window of a bakery. Umele's eye aims directly into the window. Brown shiny loaves and white roundish rolls are set out for display. Avremele had discovered that treasure yesterday, when the mother happened to leave the chamber door ajar. And what a treasure! If you really squeezed your eye right up close to the crevice you could see clearly: roundish fresh loaves and wholesome light rolls. There might have been four loaves lying in the window and perhaps ten or more rolls. Right now the sun happened to be just opposite the window, shedding its light directly on the treasures. Umele is taking it all in with his left eye, his tongue is swimming in sweet saliva. When the left eye tires he switches to the right, then back to the left, and still later back to the right. Suddenly he sees a hand inside the store removing one of the loaves. He lets out a sigh.

Behind him stands Perele, tugging at his hand. She nags:

"Let me look, let me look too. I'm hungry too."

Umele doesn't budge. Suddenly, he cries out in a strange voice:

"Don't take it, don't take it, don't take it!"

Across the way the hand has once again swept away two loaves and a whole pile of rolls. A single loaf of bread and two rolls remain in the window.

Umele still can't tear himself away from the crevice.

When Perele stubbornly grabs hold of his arm and will not relent, he flares up in anger and shouts:

"I don't want to and that's it. Leave me alone."

Through the crevice that Perele has been looking out of, one can see a little shop. Laid out majestically in the display window is a pure white cheese, nothing else. It is possible, by raising oneself a little higher on one's toes, to see part of a field, where a cow is grazing. From Umele's vantage point there is only bread and rolls. Umele stands praying to God not to let the hand reappear. He murmurs a verse his father taught him long before the ghetto. And that fragment has to accomplish everything. If you are ill, it can help; if you are very hungry and you say it with real feeling— your hunger disappears in the wink of an eye. Umele earnestly recites that holy verse now, and waits. The loaves and rolls are so close now, almost within reach. He can even see, at this point, two little holes in the bread. And he notices that a fly has alighted on one of the rolls, a huge fly with large shimmering wings.

"Umele, would you like some cheese?" Perele does not stop her nagging. "Let me in, let me in. If you don't Mama will. . . ."

God forbid that Mama should find out about this. No, Mama must not know about this, because if she does, then the whole treasure is lost. It will no longer be possible to come into the little chamber and gorge oneself on rolls and loaves of white bread. Okay, he'll let her in just for a short while, only a minute.

"Not for a long stay, Perele, all right? I don't like cheese." He moves away slowly and peeps through the other crevice.

Through the crevices the eye can escape into a free, uncaged world. Just a single leap over the fence and you are free. You can go wherever you want: to the courtyard, from the courtyard to the open fields, from the fields to the forest, further and further. The childish eyes float out of the little chamber. First of all, across the road into the shops. Now Umele can see the flat white cheese, Perele the last shiny rolls. How those rolls laugh their way right up to the children; they come so close to the crevice, so close to the eye, that Perele actually licks her little lips. You can smell the sweetness of the rich black poppy seeds. Perele's lips are already tasting the sweetness, and just look, she runs her tongue across her lips and really—she feels as if she has taken a lick of those sweetish poppy seeds.

Suddenly Perele lets out a scream. Across the street, the hand has just pulled the last of the bread and rolls out of the window. . . . Now the window is empty. Umele runs over to the crack— and he sees that the window opposite has really become a complete void.

Perele watches Umele sink to the ground, tears running down his cheeks. She is standing at her own crevice, and in the field she sees a cow with black spots.

Perele turns her head back into the chamber. She feels something soft sliding around in her throat interfering with her breathing.

"Umele," she asks, "would you like to look at some cows?"

When Umele fails to answer she sits down next to him and her eyes also start to overflow. The two of them sit there for a long time, mute, while with their fingers they dig into the dark earth of the chamber floor, till the ominous dusk settles on the little roof and the mother finds them nestled against each other, fast asleep.

That day the mother sealed the door with a nail, and from that moment on all was lost. But a couple of days later something happened that made the children forget all about the treasure they used to stare at through the window.

It happened in the morning, on a day of steady soaking rain. Swollen black clouds had settled over the ghetto. The mother was occupied with something in the corner of the room, when a neighbor came running in and cried out to her in a panic: "Glikke, they've picked up Shimmele!"

At first the mother just stood there, not understanding a single word. But the neighbor poured out the whole tale in a single breath. "It has started already," she began, explaining that today they had started the first transports of Jews, picking up people in the streets and loading them into wagons. At that point the mother went limp, right where she was standing, rolling her head and fainting dead away on the spot.

Now the panic really started. More than half the men who lived in the court, who had just happened to be out on the street, were missing. But that was just a prologue to the awesome black days that were about to descend on the ghetto.

That same evening, Mama Glikke can be seen going around with a wet compress wrapped around her head. The window, draped in black, looks like a mirror covered to protect the soul of a corpse lying in the room. The father's *tallis* and *tefillin* hang in shame in a corner. Who needs them now? Who will now bind the thongs around the arm? The mother walks in circles all day, eyes swollen with weeping. The children drag around behind her, desperately hungry. Suddenly, the mother reminds herself of something. A ray of joy creeps into her swollen eyes. From a remote nook of the room she takes out a whole loaf of bread and lays it on the table. That bread lights up the entire room, as if the sun has just flared above the horizon. She plunges the dark knife deliberately into the firm body of the bread and, swallowing the renewed flow of salty tears streaming down her cheeks, she keeps up an uninterrupted monologue:

"Eat, children, eat. It is your father's bread, your father's whole loaf of bread. . . ."

And for the first time in many, many months, the children joyfully eat to their hearts' content, as does Mama Glikke.

That night they all sleep peacefully and soundly, and Father, Shimmele, appears only to Umele in a dream. Umele sees him praying over a large, thick book.

Łódź Ghetto, 1943

❖

The Sampolne Rebbe

Last year there was no summer at all in the ghetto. Soon after Pesach an ice-cold wind suddenly started blowing again. Sterile clouds floating by left a trace of sickly pallor in the hollow sky. Winter refused to loose its grip, and ever since Hannukah a gray mist of evaporating snow remained suspended over the rooftops. People thought that as soon as the sun grew stronger, the mist would disappear and the blue sky would emerge. But well into summer the sky was still not to be seen. At the crack of dawn, when the sun was just coming over the horizon, then just barely, perhaps, for a split second, it might be possible to catch a hint of a shred of blue sky. But in an instant the shred of blue would dissolve in a blast of demonic wind bringing down a curtain of soot. The diabolically frigid wind blew freely through the window frames and attic openings. Jews who had discarded their heavy winter clothes now retrieved them from their bench-chests and once again started looking for something to chop into kindling. The sun did not show itself in this ghetto for whole days at a time. Only a bleak darkness sifted through to the streets. Each day the twilight grew denser. Once in a while a yellowish spot with vivid reddish edges, resembling an enormous glowing brass coin, would break through the clouds, then slowly slide into obscurity, as if in an eclipse.

A feeling of terror settled down on the Jews who remained in the little street, but the terror was accompanied by a desperate hope that ultimately they would be comforted. Reading some of the ancient mystical Jewish texts that had been preserved, someone had ascertained that in this very year there would be a great upheaval and disruption among the angels that would lead to the dissolution of the world. All this was to happen at a time when the Jews were going through great troubles and persecution. By means of certain allusions and numerological speculations, it was discovered that this fated year would begin with the disappearance of summer. First, there would be days that were short and truncated. The sun would appear only fitfully before being extinguished altogether. It would hang like a feeble lamp in a void among the desolate angels. Birds in mid-flight would descend to earth like falling stones.

There was a second sect of Jews on the same street who said just the opposite: the sun would indeed no longer be seen and would appear to be extinguished. But by manipulating certain texts and interpreting various biblical sayings, the sages of this sect demonstrated that these signs would only be an indication that the world is on the verge of the great moment of destruction when there would be days with no light. The sun would appear to be dead. The stars would disappear from the firmament. Powerful blizzards accompanied by thunder and lightning would break out. But all these happenings would be signs of a new beginning. ... And all these things would surely come to pass at a time when Jews are in deepest distress. And in the year of greatest Jewish suffering, a dazzling light would appear in the east with the morning stars. And that light would come like a flame which would eliminate all evil from the world, uprooting Satan and all the slaughterers of the Jewish people. The seeming destruction would actually be the moment of illumination and redemption. ...

In the peculiar weather of that summer, women and elderly Jews of the little ghetto street actually saw all manner of signs that had already been set forth in the sacred books. The decrees of the Germans had plunged the Jews into their moment of deepest darkness. Everywhere one looked, abandoned courtyards were laid waste and resembled houses for purifying the dead. Naked corpses lay rotting and unattended in the open air, and no one came to pick them up. Dead people sat at tables, leaning on their elbows, as if they were in a trance. Near their gray, lifeless heads lay dried-up potato peels.

At the first sign of sunset the few Jews left on the street used to steal into the Sampolne Rebbe's room to recite evening prayers in secret. In a double wall in his apartment, the Sampolne Rebbe had hidden a miniature Torah, which was wrapped in a blue velvet mantle studded with a variety of glowing stones. Nobody knew where the old man had obtained the miniature Torah. People whispered that all the auguries and prophecies were coming from the old man himself, from the Sampolne Rebbe. At every prayer session he used to preach good tidings to the Jews, reading prophecies of redemption out of the sacred texts. . . .

The Rebbe of Sampolne was sitting alone in his room, bent over a crumbling, dusty book. There was nothing in the room but a bucket of water and, in a corner, a bench with three legs. The fourth leg was a stack of red bricks. A fat old cat that had been following the Rebbe around for the last few months was seated on the window sill. At night the cat, lying next to his skinny feet, would even share the Rebbe's dreams. The whole thing was bizarre, since there were no cats at all in the ghetto, and yet this cat had waxed fat and flourished with the Sampolne Rebbe. The Rebbe always slept in his stockings, with the sack for his prayer shawl open at his side. He used to rouse himself suddenly out of his sleep, throw the prayer shawl over his shoulders, and suddenly start raising a racket. He roared, shouted, and stamped his feet on the floor. Neighbors would wake from their sleep, thinking the Germans were dragging Jews out into the courtyard again. But the Rebbe did not shout long, because his strength would fail him and his weak heart couldn't stand the strain. He would start to cry and would collapse like a weak newborn lamb. The cat would remain wrapped around his feet, wailing like a child. The Sampolne Rebbe would stand next to the window, supporting himself with both hands on the window frame, and look at the stars. Then he would throw open the window and stretch out both his long yellow waxen arms, which resembled two Day-of-Atonement candles.

"Gevald, sweet Father! . . . How long? How long? I ask You! . . . How long must I, the Sampolne Rebbe, pound on Your gates of mercy? Gevald, sweet Father! Gevald!"

For a long time he stood there at the window, wrapped in his prayer shawl, and shouted through the courtyard to the stars.

Long before the war had started, Jews had considered the Sampolne Rebbe something of a scatterbrain. When someone used to visit him he would first start shaking the visitor and would then honor him with a few fiery slaps. After a while he would take a peasant fiddle with three strings out of the closet and play a lovely melody. As he played, the Sampolne Rebbe kept yelling:

"Jackass! . . . Peasant dunce! . . . Do you not hear the melody of the Messiah descended from David?"

Then a little later he would throw the visitor out of the house to the accompaniment of a few blows.

The more the Sampolne Rebbe punched people and chased them from his presence, the more the Jews flocked to him, if only to hear his fiddling. There were some who claimed that after they heard his fiddle playing, their hearts opened. A festive light illuminated their entire inner being. But most of the Jews would have none of it. They concluded that the Sampolne Rebbe was simply a madman. Or else they suspected him of being involved in some sort of black magic.

As the yellowish twilight of the ghetto grew denser, the Sampolne Rebbe gave orders to pack up what little remained of Jewish artifacts, make small bundles, and prepare for great happenings. Jews said that at night they clearly saw in the dark sky how the great stars in the west were extinguished one at a time and then disintegrated. They fell in tiny fragments over the abyss where the ghetto was located.

The thirteenth day of the month of Sivan began in denser darkness than any of the preceding days of the month. The paltry light of dawn quickly melted, and at high noon deepest night returned. A persistent darkness shuffled into the remotest corners of the ghetto. The sun never rose. All the Jews of the street ran through the backyards to the Sampolne Rebbe. Women wanted to start a loud wailing, but when they saw the Rebbe's room filled with people, and the Rebbe himself pacing the room in his high white stockings, they fell mute. The crowd that had gathered in the little room was in a state of high excitement. Recognizing the truth in all of his prognostications, the Jews now gathered around the Sampolne Rebbe and looked submissively into his distorted pale face, which was flushed with the flame of an inner unearthly ecstasy. Under his torn smock, the trousers kept falling down over his white socks. As he bent over to lift his trousers, he got stuck, and remained stooped over for a long time, as if crying into his lap. At the same time, the yellow star on his shoulder started glowing with a beautiful golden radiance. The room was so dark now that the people inside couldn't see each other's faces. Children in their mother's arms started crying and whining, "Mama." The people in the room were so tightly squeezed together they had to stand on one foot. Outside, the darkness threatened like a disheveled witch. The Sampolne Rebbe tossed the prayer shawl over his shoulders, and lifting the Torah above the heads of the people shouted in a hoarse voice:

"Jews, be prepared! Let us go, let us all go! . . . Brace yourselves, Jews! . . . We are leaving right now. . . . Let us all leave together! . . . Follow me, Jews!"

He was the first one out. The rest of the crowd walked behind him under the lightless sky, treading on the stones in fearful silence. Not a pinpoint of sun came from above. They formed a long line because the street was a narrow one that ended in a high dark wall. The Sampolne Rebbe stayed in the lead, still carrying the miniature Torah. The crowd, following him through a narrow door, was now walking on soft earth. Nobody knew why they suddenly stopped on the barren ground that led to the cemetery. They realized where they were when women falling in their flight found themselves holding onto tombstones. Frightened, they ran closer to the old man from Sampolne and began shouting:

"Sampolne Rebbe! . . . Where are you taking us? Sampolne Rebbe! . . . Turn back, don't go there. . . . That's where the barbed wire is! . . . Sampolne Rebbe! . . . Sampolne Rebbe! . . ."

But the Sampolne Rebbe no longer heard anything the women shouted to him. He just kept walking with the Torah enfolded in his arms and began singing a melody in muffled tones. It was an old traditional melody—and several Jews started singing along with him in the darkness. All of a sudden a cold, frosty wind started blowing. Snow even started to fall. Tiny flakes studded the Jews' heads, like a sprinkling of silver coins. A streak of green light sliced through the darkness of the fenced-in field. The Jews walked in narrow paths among the ancient Jewish tombstones.

The snowstorm and the lightning were the last of the signs contained in the sacred texts. By this time the Sampolne Rebbe was carrying a child in one arm and the wrapped Torah in the other. He was dancing, while shouting to those behind him:

"Jews, don't be frightened! . . . Just look around you—all fences are falling! . . . All boundaries are disappearing! . . . With determination, Jews, we are getting out! . . . Out! . . . Out! . . . Look, there are no more fences! . . . Jews, sing all praise to the Creator of the Universe!"

And, indeed, the Sampolne Rebbe was the first to set foot on the little patch of ground near the old fallen gravestones. But he suddenly slipped, and as he was falling banged his head on one of the stones. He immediately regained his feet and kept on going. Another streak of lightning lit up the burial mounds. Green flashes of light snaked out of the darkness. The snow flurry swirled around them. Now the Sampolne Rebbe could see distinctly the shadows rising from death mounds—men, women, and children, some still in their loose-fitting death shrouds and others completely naked. They were all moving eastward. Another flash of lightning lit up the sky behind the throng. They kept moving forward, faster, drenched in a shimmering green light.

Łódź Ghetto, 1943

❖

Light from the Abyss

The mother and daughter bore a close resemblance to each other, and though there was a substantial age difference between them, both had gray hair and both walked with bowed heads. The mother, however, was thinner and taller, and her Adam's apple swung back and forth in her scrawny neck like a pendulum in an old-fashioned clock. Zelda's naturally flat bosom, which had never palpitated with feminine warmth, was now more sunken in than ever, and her sallow skin exuded a widow's mourning. Mother and daughter were about the same size and wore each other's clothes. Their outfits always betrayed grim sadness and an impenetrable loneliness. Their faces were bloodless and painfully pale. To add to their misery, the dwelling they had just moved into was a cramped corner of an inhospitable room full of thin spiders and gray spider webs. No matter how many of them the mother crushed, and no matter how assiduously she wiped away the webs—the next day they were hanging in the same spots, spinning their mysterious gray nets, filling that void of a room with a ghostly web that hung constantly over the heads of the mother and daughter.

From the window of this apartment, more accurately described as a little hallway facing the courtyard, it was possible to see the garden. Actually, it wasn't really a garden, just three solitary stunted trees that had stationed themselves, no one knew exactly how, on that hard, forsaken bit of earth. The trees were surrounded by a wasteland. The emptiness of the courtyard, with its dried-out, dead well, which had long since stopped giving water, made itself felt through their window. Actually, for weeks after they had moved in they did not even open the window. Locked in, hidden, the mother and daughter lay on the one bed they had rescued from the city, ashamed to look into each other's eyes. Without words, without speaking, they plunged into trivial everyday tasks. In truth, the secret of that salvaged bed was the cause of their bitter silence. Every once in a while Zelda would station herself at either the head or foot of the bed and stroke her gray neck with her yellow hands—careful not to let her mother see. Her eyes then bulged, and she stood there as if turned to stone. Once again she saw everything exactly as it had happened. She had spent many long months before the war preparing for her wedding. Basic household needs had been purchased for her: linen for shirts and pillow cases, and all sorts of domestic goods. And Leibush, the groom, a carpenter by trade, had prepared a wardrobe and bed with his own hands.

The bed was the first item finished, a wide, stately affair with a high, corniced headboard. For many long months it waited, fully assembled, in a corner of her mother's house. The day of the wedding ceremony drew near, but the Germans reached the gates of the city before it arrived. In the ensuing chaos, Leibush left with the rest of the city's fleeing refugees and did not return. Now the mother and daughter had been hounded into this little corner. At the last moment they had grabbed whatever they could, a few bits of clothing left over from Zelda's wedding trousseau, and the wedding bed itself. For weeks it stood disassembled, while the mother and Zelda lay on the floor, using their clothes as bedding. Later on, when the cold weather arrived, and winter set in, the mother set up the bed. They lay there staring at the rafters and into the remote corners of the room, watching grotesque spiders weave their cloth. From beyond the walls the crying of young children broke the silence. And sometimes loud lamentations for deceased neighbors who had left the world as swollen hulks forced their way into the apartment and clung to the walls, ringing in their ears through long hours of silence, like the hum of noisy crickets.

At first, the mother would not sleep in the bed. She refused to get into it, and for many weeks she slept in a corner of the room, using tablecloths and clothes as her bedding. Her mother's avoidance of the bed made Zelda even more keenly aware of the all-encompassing misery of her young shattered life. But after they had been in the apartment for a while, Zelda called out to her mother in a soft voice shaky with tears:

"I know everything, Mother. I know everything. . . . The dead never return. . . . He will never come back. . . . Never!"

It was then that the mother realized that Zelda had already dealt with her loss in her own way, and that she had overcome the grief in her heart.

Winter that year was unusually cruel, frigid blue days bloated with hunger. Jews lay in their beds around the clock, while the snow and frost danced merrily at their windows. The blackened faces of the elderly, who resembled sick children, peeped out of the dark pillows they had managed to hang on to. The three death wagons that harvested the dead and frozen from their apartments raced through the narrow streets like driven demons. Each wagon, with a huge crate set on top, made a racket as it clattered down the streets. The crate would rock, first right, then left. Soon it would fall off the wagon and spill the naked corpses in the snow. The frost cut like an executioner's whetted blade. Youngsters came running out of houses, carrying wooden boards from which corpses would be unloaded. The snow dropped gently on the stiff emaciated bodies as the young people pitched them into the crates. No relatives were at hand. Somewhere in the courtyard an abrupt human scream would sink into the void. The wind, reaching right up to the huge, open crate, tossed frosty mounds of snow directly onto the faces of the corpses.

The ghetto courtyards are empty.

Zelda and her mother have been lying in bed since last night. A biting cold penetrates the little windows. The windowpanes are draped in gray shirts of ice. The mother naps, hunger gnawing at her heart. All at once, a gravelly voice shouts from the other side of the wall:

"Geva-a-a-ald! . . . Sa-a-a-ave me! Geva-a-a-ald!"

Feet shuffle behind the wall. Someone starts chanting Psalms in a loud voice. Then silence. A minute later the chanting can be heard again, along with a typically Yiddish sighing, the unique sighing with which Jews always express their grief in the face of death.

A little later, the scenario is repeated, but this time the screaming from behind the wall is much louder and lasts for a long time. Zelda and her mother sit up in the bed. The screaming continues without letting up. It is probably a lament for someone who has just died. What can be done? It is as freezing in the room as in the courtyard. The water in the pots on the stove is frozen solid. The floor has a bluish tint, and the light that filters through the coated windowpanes gives it the appearance of cold glass. On the walls, thousands of little diamonds glitter in the blue winter light.

Just before evening the door opens, and Reb Asher appears in the doorway. He is the only neighbor on the other side of the wall. In a torn winter jacket and wide wooden shoes, his skinny blue feet sticking out of them, he stands there mumbling, his lips moving without uttering anything coherent. Then he looks into the room and, seeing the two women huddled together in bed, turns and leaves.

It was not until the next morning that Zelda paid a visit to the neighbor.

The room was unusually dark; the one small window was heavily coated with ice. The room was completely bare, without a table, without a chair, without a bed. The only objects in the room were some tightly tied bundles of old clothes in the corners. Someone was lying on a pile of straw, covered with old clothes. Rabbi Asher was sitting on a heap of bricks near the man lying on the straw. He was bent over a book, reading silently, moving his lips but making no sound. The person in the straw, tall and emaciated, looked like a wisp of straw himself. His yellow sunken face blended perfectly with the straw pillow on which it lay. The eyes peering out of that face were large and still animated. When Zelda entered the room, the old man turned his face toward the door, and then instantly turned back to the person lying at his side:

"Leibush, take a look. . . . We have a visitor. . . . Open your eyes. . . . Open . . ."

Zelda felt a stab of pain in her heart.

Leibush? How strange . . . In a flash she recognized the eyes of her lost groom. A pair of mysterious warm hands grabbed her skinny shoulders and led her closer to the "bed." The old man stood up and told her to sit.

"Sit down, neighbor. Though we don't have a single chair. That's the fate that has befallen us. Such a fate. Not even a little warm food for someone who is dying."

Meanwhile, the bundle of black clothes moved slightly. Two green flames that were actually a pair of human eyes gazed out of the pillow. The bundle breathed heavily.

"A neighbor? From next door?"

Zelda listened carefully to his voice, which was soft and warm. She nodded her head slightly, but the man lying in the straw did not see the gesture, the encroaching evening having swallowed up every movement.

A little later the old man went out and left Zelda alone with his son.

He had gone to look for a few scraps of wood for a fire, so he could cook some warm food. He was away for a long time, leaving the two young people sitting in the darkness. And in that cold darkness, in that frost-filled room, its walls decorated with silvery ice-molds, Zelda, attending the sick person lying in the straw, felt her shriveled heart melt. She stretched her hand toward him to cover his exposed shoulder, and her fingers felt the warmth leaving his bony body.

Under the sickly flowers of glistening frost blossoming on the walls Leibush lay a mass of swollen flesh. He extended his warm soft hand from under the tattered clothes and laid it on Zelda's skinny knee, letting it rest there a long time. Zelda felt that this person who had been a stranger to her just a moment ago, and who would probably die soon, had instantaneously become a more intimate companion to her than her mother. The young man was burning with fever and breathed fitfully. She would have given the little warmth left in her own heart just to set him on his feet. Her maidenly yearnings had been gradually extinguished by her shattered life, but now a tiny bit of ash that had somehow remained glowing in an unknown corner of her being projected a radiant warmth through the yellow skin of her breast. She no longer felt cold or hungry; gone were the evil days, and the icicles around her heart melted like ice floes under a warm sun. Something noble struggled to assert itself within her emaciated frame. In that dark room of blossoming ice-flowers, holding Leibush's sickly hand on her knees, Zelda's splintered heart was made whole. She felt ashamed of her thoughts and of the warmth that suffused her being. Leibush kept his eyes closed and did not take his hands off her. As she sat there, a thought stole slowly into Zelda's consciousness. Laying her thin hand on his burning face, she bent over him and stammered in a low voice:

"Leibush, you are going to recover, you'll see; I am going to bring you back to health. . . . Leibush . . . Leibush . . ." And then she ran out.

She looked around the room. Her mother was still lying in the big bed, asleep. A frozen moon peered through the windowpane, casting a green glow on the walls. Zelda searched for something in the corners. She was possessed by a single thought: wood. She had to find wood to heat the apartment in which Leibush was lying, to cook some warm food, to heat compresses for his feet. If only there were a chair in the room, or a little wardrobe, she would have hacked it into kindling wood and started a fire. She looked around the room again, and saw nothing but the bed, her own great wedding bed with the high cornices.

She has an idea: chop up the bed. She looks for the ax. It is a heavy, sharp ax. She can barely lift it. Her mother opens one eye and watches Zelda's fussing. Completely engrossed, Zelda is stalking around the bed. Her mother thinks Zelda has gone mad. Half frozen and still half asleep, the mother can't figure out what is happening. With a sudden movement, Zelda raises the ax and brings it down on the headboard of the bed. The ax remains stuck in the cleft, but the bedstead is dislodged. She snatches the ax out of the wood, and in one hard push the cornice is lying on the floor. She grabs it and splits it into smaller pieces. Her hands loaded down with the chips of wood, she runs into Leibush's room. She quickly sits down on the ground near the stove, and in a moment, a weak fire has pushed back the frosty darkness. From time to time she leaves the stove, runs to the dark corner where Leibush is lying, and utters breathlessly:

"Soon, Leibush, soon. Soon it will be warm, soon you will have a hot compress. . . . You'll have some grits."

Now the dry wood of the large cornice is blazing, and the

smoke spreads a warm spell through the room. Reb Asher sits on the bricks chanting psalms. Zelda puts up a pot of water. She lifts her dull eyes and thinks they see miraculous new things. The room fills with the echoes of a chorus singing psalms. The blossoming flowers on the walls change colors kaleidoscopically; pearls of dew tell of the coming of sunny summer days. Out of the warmth spreading to every corner of the room from the old man's chanting of psalms and the cold flowers on the wall emerges an enchanted light fluttering over an abyss.

Łódź Ghetto, 1943

❂

Ghetto Kingdom

A streak of light slices through the night sky, cutting through clouds resembling tattered black garments. It's as if the retiring genie of night has lashed the intermittent clouds with a birch whip, leaving a bloody strip of light running the length of the eastern horizon. As the light diffuses into innumerable red tassels, strands of thread, and polka dots, the swollen, dark clouds retreat shamefacedly. A predawn wind from out of nowhere that has somehow ridden the grayish morning light into the ghetto suddenly assaults the clouds, which dissipate into countless fragments of color. In the east, poised on the edge of day and night, the ruddy dome of the sun hangs on the rooftops, as the remaining clouds gradually melt away.

Night still blankets the ghetto, as though daylight is ashamed to show its face on the mute wooden thresholds, and when the light of dawn creeps into the crumbling aged walls of Balut, it shimmers strangely and darkly, like a hearse spreading dismay among mourners.

No sooner has the sickly daylight made its way into the ghetto than people start stirring in the semidarkness, streaming into the streets from under stairways, from dark cellars, from tiny apartments now occupied by formerly rich city folk hanging on to the possessions they had salvaged—people with little sacks, hand-stitched packets, and purses—all wrapped together and squeezed under their arms. Pouring out of all the buildings, out of every room, out of every hole, with their sacks and packages clutched to their hearts, these people fan out across the ghetto courtyards. Like a flock of frightened mice drawn to slimy decaying garbage, they descend in multitudes on any kind of grayish refuse, on the sticky filth rotting in both the exposed and concealed garbage cans of the Ghetto Kingdom.

A stench rises from the garbage cans, which have attracted the attention of the mice-people; the cans are filled with putrefaction, disease, and decay. The garbage cans of the Ghetto Kingdom are indicative that anything thrown away in the ghetto is already hardly more than excrement. For who in this place would discard anything that could still be chewed, or transformed in various mysterious ways into a "tasty" morsel? In any given rubbish heap there are only sticky rags and putrefied scraps; not even a potato peel can be found in the garbage, because in recent days the demon hunger has invented a new devil's delicacy.

Someone steps up to the town well and stealthily, yet with uncanny strength, starts rubbing something under the cold streams of water flowing from the well. A master chef has discovered that leftover potato peels washed and ground can be transformed, as if by sheer magic, into flat cutlets; this sticky, cloying delicacy is as sweet as a piece of fine cake, though the sand that hasn't been washed away by the water grates between the teeth. But who cares about that? The demon hunger renders the delicacy a savory meal to the sick and swollen, magically converting it into the wheat bread they have been dreaming of.

It is twelve noon. An exhausted sun sags limply in the narrow streets. The crowd is returning, walking through the open courtyards, a kind of green agonized gleam concealed in their eyes. In the bundles and little sacks they are carrying the rottenness that is tearing their guts apart. They toss their gleanings onto the table. The children descend on the garbage. A mother plunges her skinny hands into the filth and searches. Her fingers have found something—something dark and slimy. A fiendish green glint slides across her sunken cheeks.

The room swims around her as if she were in a strange country, on another planet, under another sky dotted with multitudes of rising stars. The sickly light of dawn is no longer suspended outside the window. Good tidings warming their hungry tummies are wafted from a hidden fire. The delicacy in the children's little hands is hot and burning, black and dark.

On the site of the great market, which used to overflow with fresh greens and nourishing foodstuffs before the murderous war, there are now strange people selling gooey, withered victuals dyed with some sort of unnatural greenness. A few women, looking like hungry cats and sticking out the tips of their tongues, are standing around a little table. Next to the table, bread is being sold, not loaves, but crumbled, mealy, tiny scraps that are moldy and sopping with moisture. These are the portions of bread that make up the ration allotted to each person. Those selling the bread stand with heads bowed in their dark kerchiefs that display threadbare gold Star of David patches; they resemble transmogrified souls who have come here to serve as a reminder of the destruction of the Temple. They look at the holy bread through half-shut eyes; their breasts, which gave suck to weak Jewish babes, sag. Occasionally, they let out a wail, as if at a funeral.

A Jew is shuffling around. In his hand he holds three potatoes, two of which are completely wholesome; the third is rotten. A small crowd of Jews is gathering around him, gazing at the treasure. The Jew does not let the potatoes out of his hand. Anybody who wants to buy them will have to do so without touching them. Nobody takes them. But it is good just to look at a potato, a real potato. . . .

Children are milling around among the adults as the women holding them by the hand try to drag them home. The women themselves, as they walk through the marketplace, think back to those bygone years when the market was packed with nutritious foodstuffs.

As if by some miracle, the marketplace fills up with peasant wagons, with little pushcarts, and covered booths. On the wagons, amid open sacks bulging with greens, amid potatoes and red beets, amid haphazard piles of mushrooms, sit slobbering peasants. Young gentile boys are standing on other wagons, cracking their whips to chase the little thieves who are trying to sneak under the wheels. Rows of women are sitting along both sides, with juicy radishes and hefty heads of cabbage smiling out of the little sacks tucked between their parted knees. A village scent of horse stalls and warm manure hovers in the air.

A Jewish woman is walking by, when all of a sudden she

grasps her throat, as if she is choking from the smoke, and in the blink of an eye two Jewish men are carrying her away—unconscious.

The red gate of Holy Mary Church is located right behind the market. Fenced in, trapped inside the Jewish ghetto, the abandoned church stands silent. In the crevices of its walls reside the ghosts of forgotten generations. The low fence that runs around the church has somehow sunk lower. The great iron doors, rusted by rain and wind, are now always open. Jews in down-covered smocks and women wearing traditional kerchiefs run back and forth along the cool, empty church corridors. Here the white down and soft feathers of Jewish bedding are packed. The down and feathers, stained with blood and dampened with Jewish tears, have been brought from the surrounding hamlets. The Jews run around the church, looking as if they have been dipped in snow. High in the belfry the church clock has stopped telling time, and only the wind can be heard whistling around the gigantic bells. Various holy saints are standing on the sills of the narrow windows, looking down with tearful gilded eyes at the Jews running about below. A golden light seems to descend from their round faces and the sunny halos around their heads as a zephyr stirs among the bells.

While the large gray sacks are being packed with soft down, a barely audible ringing seems to be coming from on high. The damped ringing actually does come from above, from the towers where the hitherto mute bells have broken their silence. Eerily and mysteriously, they have started swinging. The Jews are afraid to raise their heads as the bells swing more vigorously, swelling into a powerful song that carries to the outer reaches of the nearby fields. Soon the peasants will be coming. The belfry is filled with pious music. The long corridors resound with humble and pious footsteps. The Jews do not lift their heads; a fear of churchly shadows descends into their hearts. They gather into a corner and one of the group gives vent to an enormous sigh:

"Master of the Universe, be merciful to your people, Israel. . . . Have pity on your wretched people! . . ."

And from above, from the high, empty towers, once again the sound of the cold, lonely wind.

Evening. The market and "Holy Mary" church are enveloped in a blue twilight mist. In the empty plaza around the church, the chestnut trees are raising an uncanny racket, as if they are enchanted. The streets are emptying out. Somewhere in the nearby fields the genie of night waits once again, wrapping within his hands the last choking breath of day. For Jews the curfew hour has started.

On a side street not far from the church is a small brick chapel with an "eternal light" burning inside, and above the light a plaster statue of the Crucified One. The darker it gets outside, the more vivid glows the red light beneath the Crucified One. Once again the wind whistles around the tower clock. Night has already fallen on the windows of the Ghetto Kingdom. The holy flame from the little chapel lashes the face of the last Jew as he runs through the narrow street. Boots are pounding on the other side of the wire. Germans are entering the ghetto. The Crucified One in the heart of the ghetto is now drenched in flame. His thin tortured Jewish body lies curled in a red pool of warm blood.

Łódź Ghetto, 1943

❖

Enchanted Fruit

Spring had barely begun when it became apparent that the coming summer would be a hot one filled with "blessings." After a snowy winter, unmistakable signs of spring had finally appeared: the sky over the ghetto was luxuriant and deep, casting a mild barely remembered light on the ghetto below. But the clearest indication of spring was the fresh growth, the little patches of green that struggled through the barren ground. Joyful greens and a spectrum of bright colors had burst into the open. Overnight, scraggly bushes were clothed in shirts of green velvet. Strange song birds, not the usual sparrows, came flying into the ghetto. Hidden in the lilac bushes inside the barbed wire around the ghetto, they joined the ghetto sparrows in singing. They poured forth a stream of song that told of a young forest wind originating somewhere, and of a lightness of spring being born.

The closer you came to the cemetery, the more clearly you could see the onset of summer. The gray death-field had turned into a garden where the dead slept peacefully under the flower beds. Rows of ancient Polish trees lined both sides of the sandy fields: tall poplars next to pointy-leafed maples; weeping willows and reddish chestnut trees. Bushes with leafy twigs whose green shoots were once used to help celebrate Shavuous* in Jewish homes hugged the ground. The path leading to the last resting place of the dead was the only street to have turned green. The black wagons made their way along that same green path day after day, from sunrise till the stars disappeared from the heavens. Since they were never accompanied by mourners, the wagons

---

* Literally [the Feast of] Weeks, this holiday occurs sometime at the end of May or the beginning of June and celebrates the giving of the Torah at Sinai. It is also a celebration of the Festival of the First Fruits.

made their way along the lonely path speedily, passing under the spreading trees now in bloom. White blossoms, recently emerged greenish buds, and bright green succulent leaves rained down on the roofs of the black wagons, where the angular faces and bloated bodies of the dead rested under a large black sheet. Once on hallowed ground, the grave diggers had to shake out the black cover sheet thoroughly, so thickly were all its folds strewn with delicate blossoms.

Spring had been fleeting, and summer followed hard upon winter. Jewish grave diggers saw the hallowed ground turn green overnight. One morning they went to the cemetery before dawn to prepare the daily graves, only to find the entire area green, as if it were already after Shavuous. Days later, as if by some miracle, raspberries appeared on the bushes near the tombstones, at first a pale green, then a light red. It did not take long for the "blessed" raspberry bushes to cloak themselves in berries. Cemetery raspberries are always slightly different from those in forests or open fields, but this year the berries grew so fast that they were noticeably different, even from the usual cemetery raspberries. This time they were a peculiarly vivid red; they were huge and soft-fleshed, and at the slightest touch, left a dark crimson stain on the finger. Having ripened so early, they hung over the sandy death-mounds like multitudes of red stars.

In their constant digging, the grave diggers would now and then take a swipe at the raspberry bushes with their sharp spades, even though they could be punished for doing so. They would stuff fistfuls of raspberries into their open mouths till the deep red fluid overflowed their lips and dribbled down their chins. They also used to fill their pockets with raspberries and smuggle them into the ghetto. Guards were posted at many points around the cemetery to keep an eye on the raspberry bushes, because all the fields of innumerable raspberries were the property of one Jew—The Eldest of the Jews of the Litzmannstadt Ghetto.

Only one of the old grave diggers had managed to survive—fat Kiel, my mother's younger brother. Before taking over the trade of grave digging from old Great-Uncle Pinchas, he had made a living, in partnership with some Christian boys, by keeping pigeons in his little room in Balut. When he rode over to the annual farmer's market to buy new pigeons from the peasants, he would always take along a few pigeons that had already been fattened up at home, and when he got to the market he would turn them loose. The pigeons always returned to Balut, a feat Uncle Kiel was very proud of. After he married and his wife died unexpectedly, he got rid of the pigeons, because, to tell the truth, he was heartbroken. Then, after Uncle Kiel's wife had been buried, old Great-Uncle Pinchas, who was in charge of all cemetery business, invited Uncle Kiel to his room and ordered his daughter, Chava, to set out some honey cake and whiskey. Gossip has it that it was at that meeting that old Great-Uncle Pinchas arranged for the two of them to be married. Whether or not that's how it happened I can't say because I was never able to verify the story. But the fact remains that soon after his wife died, Uncle Kiel remarried and took over the undertaking business.

Old Great-Uncle Pinchas, who still remembered the time of the cholera epidemic, died soon after the wedding. He was already well into his eighties. The grave diggers in my family all died at a ripe old age. The old man instructed Uncle Kiel in all the subtleties of the grave digger's trade. He taught him how to recite the *El Malei Rachamim** prayer, how to set up a tombstone, how to distinguish between good dry earth fit for digging a grave and earth that would cave in because it was eroded by the subterranean streams of the Stav River. He also taught him how to wend his way through the hundreds of avenues and streets thickly overgrown with grass and weeds that snaked through the great Jewish cemetery. The first time I saw Uncle Kiel he was already in his fifties, and I had just barely started putting on *tefillin*. He lived in a red brick building with other grave diggers. The wall of that building adjoined the shed where the dead were cleansed. I remind myself now that the first time I went to the cemetery was when one of the neighbors in our courtyard died. That was the first time I witnessed a Jewish death. When they carted the black

---

* "God of Mercy," part of the daily liturgy, also included in the memorial prayer for the dead.

hearse away in the dark, shiny wagon, my youthful heart was filled with sadness and terror as I thought about my own death, which I was sure must be imminent. Worse yet, the lamentations of the family and of all the Jews who lived in that courtyard penetrated my consciousness and made me feel as if I were the corpse lying in that coffin. None of my family or neighbors noticed how I followed the hearse right onto the hallowed ground. I wanted to see the final disposition of the dead with my own eyes.

That was the first time I saw Uncle Kiel, the grave digger.

His face was ringed by a bright reddish beard that completely enveloped his broad face. The beard covered his nose, and even his temples, so you could only see his small eyes, watery and blue as two deep pools. He was tall and sturdy and had a touch of granite in his shoulders. Walking among the graves, with his coat thrown over his broad powerful shoulders, he looked like a peasant walking his land, engaged in the holy work of farming. That first time he came out along the path to meet me. He wore a round cut-out hat, and in all seasons, summer or winter, the upper part of his boots always had dried yellowish clods of earth from fresh graves clinging to them. I couldn't take my eyes off the earth stuck to his boots, which seemed to me to have come from the other world. When he talked he would always lay his hand on his face and part his wild-growing beard, disclosing his broad laughing mouth. He was always laughing, a bright ringing laugh which seemed to me at that time like some kind of enchanted laughter from the world beyond. He would stand right next to me, take me by the hand, and whisper:

"Well, do you think you would like to learn the trade of the Angel of Death?"

In Uncle Kiel's apartment there was always a warm friendly crowd of strange men and women, as if his place were an inn. These people came and went in a steady stream, into his apartment and out, from the cemetery and to the cemetery. Jews died in far-off parts of the city, and here the departed were given a decent Jewish burial. The crowd in Uncle Kiel's apartment was made up of people who made a living in the great Jewish cemetery: monument engravers and those engaged in the business of burial; receipt-writers and Psalm chanters; diggers and purifiers; paid wailing-women and the plain poor folk, who love to frequent cemeteries. Uncle Kiel's second wife, Aunt Chava, a tall spare woman with three sets of keys pushed far down into her reddish apron, was always baking honey cakes and then laying thick slices on a silver tray, to wash down the fiery moonshine that Jews in this area still drank from pot-bellied bottles. But it was not only the local inhabitants who drank. Also among the drinkers were mourners leaving the hallowed ground after a funeral, those who had come to commemorate relatives long dead, and anybody else who happened to cross my uncle's threshold. In his apartment there was always a crowd, and the place buzzed with the sounds of life. People were constantly toasting "to life," at the same time that cries of mourning could be heard coming from the purification hut. In the summer, the children of the grave diggers, of whom (may no evil eye strike them) there were multitudes, played among the tombstones; in a spirit of innocent mischief they leapt secretly over the recently prepared grave sites. At night, when a full yellowish moon shimmered above the spotty clouds and cast its enchanted night-silver over the ancient mausoleums and age-old monuments, then young adolescents would meander arm in arm among the tombs, in passionate secret love. Here, hasty weddings and circumcisions were performed. The Holy Days, and also the thirty days of mourning, were celebrated quite differently in the little cemetery synagogue than in synagogues on the other side. Because this was the domain of death, therefore it was precisely here that death did not exist. There was only the silent flight from a turbulent world to one of stillness and eternal peace.

Those were the early years of my childhood—and at that time everything still seemed strange and wonderful: how did those people, constantly surrounded by Jewish death, manage to carry on their daily lives so joyously? Actually, I discovered the answer to that question years later, during that other wonderful summer of the fourth ghetto year, when those huge red raspberries blossomed profusely among the innumerable graves.

That summer Uncle Kiel was the only prewar grave digger left among the score or so of younger grave diggers in the ghetto cemetery. By this time he had long been a widower and his only sister, Tzirel, had long been living outside the cemetery with her daughter, Mindel. Now Uncle Kiel either wandered around among the blossoming red raspberry bushes with his spade on his shoulder or else dug in the earth. The warm wind from the near-by burial grounds, which he permitted to blow freely on his unkempt beard, was like a bow on the strings of an enchanted fiddle singing of worlds long dead. During the ghetto years the burial grounds were seeded with a numerous host of Jews that extended all the way down to the road to Brzezin. It had been necessary to requisition adjoining potato fields for the cemetery from ethnic Germans, who agreed to move with pleasure. Uncle Kiel knew all the families whose members came his way one by one. He even knew which members of each family were still alive. Maybe there was a daughter still in this world, or a grandchild, and in some cases no one at all left to be buried. Though he himself was now bereft of family and descendants, he still did his work as he had performed it in years past, with purposeful dedication. The many years of his close companionship with death completely erased from his consciousness even the slightest fear of it, as if he had been groomed for eternal life. But in the fourth year of the ghetto everything suddenly changed.

The dying of Jews had become so unrelenting that death began to take on a strange and alien appearance: the corpses no longer resembled those he had returned to the earth all the years he had been a grave digger. The Jewish bodies came to him bloated and swollen, like broad tree stumps, and could hardly be squeezed into the waiting graves. Moreover, a sharp acidic odor emanated from the ragged death shrouds. Because of the malignant diseases raging in the ghetto, the Germans forbade the washing of the dead. The Jewish bodies were thrown into their graves without being given a ritual Jewish, or even a decent human, burial.

At that time, thoughts of rebellion slowly began stirring in Uncle Kiel's consciousness. It began to dawn on him that a heinous crime was being committed against the Jewish people. It is not commonly known that he once crawled among the moldy tombstones, cast himself down at the foot of a mausoleum and lay there for several days, pressing his belly into the sunken earth saturated with the moisture of rotting leaves. Then, ensconced in the darkness of the mausoleum, where gray cemetery birds nested and ancient otherworldly spiders wove their thin silvery threads, he would, from time to time, lift his face in the darkness to gaze at the eternal glow of the ancient fading Hebrew letters engraved on the stones, though the golden glitter of the engraved prayers had long been extinguished, dissolved into the stone by rain, snow, and wind. Uncle Kiel embraced the clods of earth on the grave mounds, and in the darkness of the mausoleum haltingly uttered a prayer in simple Yiddish words. That was how Uncle Kiel prayed, and as he spoke, a flickering light emanated from the graves of the dead Jews. He pleaded with the dank earth underneath him, and his muttering lips searched for some kind of revelation, a miracle to stay the plague cutting down the Jews. He even wept, stuttering through his tears, and prayed to the hallowed spirits to intercede with the Creator. All he asked was to be able to purify the dead ghetto Jews and wrap them in clean linen.

Something strange happened to Uncle Kiel right after his only sister died in the ghetto, leaving her grown daughter, Mindel, on her own. As Uncle Kiel had stood in the grave next to his sister, who was wrapped in a tattered green Sabbath tablecloth, he shouted into her swollen face: "You can rest easy, Tzirel, I'll take care of your Mindele." He even lay his finger lightly on her half-open eye, a congealed gooey pupil resembling a crushed plum. That eye smiled up at him comfortingly with a mysterious light.

When he awoke the sun was just rising, and the tearful softness of the midnight dew was still on the leaves. Bluish drifts of morning fog floated low over the fields behind the fence. They eased upward, then slowly descended to earth like pale sheer bridal veils. The sweet aroma of the raspberry bushes, intensified by the warm night rain, was being disseminated by a fresh summer breeze. As soon as the light of the last star disappeared, the early summer sun would heat the graves all the long summer day.

With his velvet prayer-shawl bag under his arm and a jar in his hand, he wandered the hallowed ground among the low raspberry bushes. He got down on his hands and knees and began picking berries one at a time. He wanted to get an early start visiting his deceased sister's daughter, Mindele, before dawn and bring her the raspberries.

He realized that he was not preparing to go from the cemetery into the ghetto just for the sake of his orphaned niece. He suddenly felt a yearning in his heart to be as close as possible to the last remnants of the Jewish community. The last two ghetto years had separated him from the fate of the Jews, and it was for that reason that he now felt drawn to all those Jews outside the cemetery. He also knew that he was going to the ghetto with still another purpose—an ulterior motive, perhaps, but one so pure that when he reminded himself of it he felt as if thin threads of holy light from the dark Jewish mausoleums were weaving their way through his aging heart.

As soon as he had filled both the jar and the prayer-shawl bag with raspberries, he headed directly for the gate leading into the ghetto.

The path from the cemetery gate to the hill that led down into the ghetto was covered with a thin layer of blossoms, some from the trees lining the path and some blown from the cemetery. In his old wrinkled boots, Uncle Kiel plowed through the scattered blossoms as though walking through newly fallen snow. The blossoms stuck to the damp clumps of earth on his boots.

Beyond the fence that enclosed the large Jewish cemetery lay the still, silent, empty ghetto neighborhoods. Though it was the month of Sivan, when the earth was supposed to be in full bloom, the ground on the other side of the cemetery was barren, as if it were not the same earth in which the dead lay sleeping. The fields here were sandy and raw, as if they contained within themselves the curse of sinning worlds. Angry birds twittered across the barren bushes that clung to the sandy ground, and chirped an unbirdlike song.

The area was located on a mountain. Facing north you could see the entire city, with its gray-topped buildings and shining church steeples, stretched out at your feet. To the south lay the ghetto quarter, enveloped in a shabby kerchief of low-lying clouds, dappled and tearful.

In the two years that my uncle had not left the cemetery, he had grown unaccustomed to coming into contact with living beings. Little by little he forgot what a living human body looked like. Day in, day out, people had to be buried, and there was no day of rest for the grave diggers, either. In unseemly haste they returned the dead to the earth—all those who had fallen and gone under were buried without being given the last rites, to which all human beings are entitled. Now, walking with his prayer-shawl bag filled with the red raspberries, he knew that he was carrying a momentous message—one that had come to him in the dark mausoleums housing the immortal holy spirits. He kept looking toward the cemetery and could not turn his eyes away. A dark warm yearning drew his encrusted heart to the death-mounds surrounded by summer blossoms. He knew that he would be returning before long. Walking along the empty path he did not meet a living soul. The further he went from the cemetery, the more he felt drawn to the ghetto. The path descended into a small street, where decayed shanties swayed along both sides of the road. Children were sitting on one of the stoops. When they saw the old man with the disheveled beard they sprang toward him, grabbed him by his fluttering coat tails, and stretched out their thin transparent hands. A pussy discharge caused by malnutrition ran from the children's eyes. Their bulging eyes glistened like the eyes of adults just before they died. He couldn't remove his gaze from the green glossiness of their eyes, which made him choke. The children were like little ghosts groveling at his feet, tearing at his coat, scrambling up his body to get to the prayer-shawl bag, which he hugged to his heart. They kept screaming in their shrill voices:

"Dear grampsy, offer us something! . . . Dear sir, give us something! . . . 'Charity will rescue from damnation!' . . . Offer something to Jewish children! . . ."

He looked around. The street was abandoned. A moldy wind reeking of death was blowing from behind the little houses and fallen picket fences. Moving very slowly, he barely managed to disentangle himself from the children's hands. Then he took them by their fingertips and led them into a dark empty corridor.

In the corridor, Uncle Kiel stuffed fistfuls of red raspberries into the children's outstretched hands. They suddenly became frightened and one by one shied away from him. They looked at the raspberries in their hands and did not know what to do with them. They brought their hands up to their noses, inhaled the aroma, and looked at the old man suspiciously. For the first time they actually saw the peculiar fruit. They hadn't really expected to get anything out of the old man, yet here, right in their hands, lay these slimy red nuggets. They started to draw back in fear. They were afraid to put them in their mouths. Then Uncle Kiel took several raspberries in his hand, muttered something to himself, and laying his hands on the children's heads, whispered in a tremulous voice:

"Children, say a blessing! It's God's bounty! Raspberries. Sweet raspberries."

The children looked at the enchanted red nuggets one more time, then raised their vacuous eyes to the old man, who was sucking the juice out of the raspberries with his aged lips.

They hurriedly started stuffing the raspberries into their parched mouths. The red juice on their lips looked like bloodstains. They immediately tasted the outlandish sweetness and stretched out their hands for more. Uncle Kiel barely managed to get away from them, for the children chased him a distance, like demons in a nightmare. He descended a twisted street into the ghetto. He had to save some fruit for Mindele. In the distance he could still see the children stretching their hands out to him and licking the redness of the crushed raspberries.

When he arrived, Mindel was airing out some old clothes left by her late mother. Uncle Kiel stood in the doorway holding his prayer-shawl bag. Mindel was a grown girl, with a small head sitting erect but rather unsteadily on her drooping shoulders. She was tall and her thin curly hair had the same dark reddish tone as Uncle Kiel's beard. Everyone in the family had that red hair.

Mindel couldn't recall Uncle Kiel's ever having come into town directly from the cemetery before. The only other occasions on which she had ever seen him were family funerals. The two years the ghetto had been in existence he had never been here before. Now, seeing this strange man standing on her doorstep, Mindel cried out in alarm. She looked at him with frightened glances. Uncle Kiel came closer to her, stretched out his hand, and said in a soft voice:

"Are you Mindel, my sister's child?"

"Uncle Kiel!" she cried, casting away the clothes and throwing herself into his outstretched hairy arms.

She burst into tears and sobbed inconsolably as he held her.

Uncle Kiel mumbled something under his beard, then slowly sat down on the edge of the bench. After a while he silently started picking the little red raspberries out of his prayer-shawl bag with searching fingers and putting them into Mindel's trembling hands. Then he walked over to the pail, poured some water, washed his hands according to ritual, and took out his prayer shawl. He cast the prayer shawl over his head and his unkempt red beard, so that his face was entirely hidden. Standing in a corner of the room he looked like a narrow bureau covered to keep off dust. The white threads of his prayer shawl were dotted here and there with red stains left by God's beautiful earthly fruit. Standing at a distance and watching in amazement as her Uncle Kiel prayed, it seemed to Mindel that the stains were little red stars in the sky, sending out red rays from an alien world no longer in existence.

The thought that he had come here on an important mission for the living lit up his heart like a glowworm punching holes of light in the darkness of night. At first he couldn't imagine what this mission would be, but now a bright light expanded in his heart like a rising sun. And that sun gradually swept aside the heavy clouds casting a shadow on his visage.

When his niece, Mindel, woke up early the next morning, Uncle Kiel was already up and about. He spoke to her, but in distant mysterious words which filled her heart with girlish fear. At first she couldn't figure out what her uncle wanted of her. As he spoke he kept running his hands through his dark red beard. He opened his eyes wider under his thick bushy eyebrows and kept repeating that "those over there," the congregation of the dead, had sent him here to carry out God's mission. She began growing more fearful of the old man who filled the small room and confused her with those strange ravings, burning words of God, of the dead, and of the holy Jewish body. In her panic she withdrew into a corner of the room and wanted to cry out, because the old man who exuded the cool scent of the dug-up earth stood over her like one possessed, his fluttering hands thrashing around like the wings of a wounded bird. She screamed in fear because Uncle Kiel's words had filled that small room with hundreds of ghosts. All of them kneeled to her, bowing their bony bodies and unbeating hearts. Finally, she simply nodded her head, and when the old man took her by the hand she allowed him to lead her, as a blind man lets himself be led by one who can see.

That same morning, Uncle Kiel and his niece, Mindel, went from house to house and apartment to apartment through the small courtyards of the ghetto. At each apartment they would inquire into the whereabouts of someone who, God forbid, had died. And when they were led to the spot where the dead person lay they began to give the corpse the last rites: they washed the dead body and clothed it with whatever they could find. They divided the work between them: Uncle Kiel busied himself with men and boys, while Mindel took care of the women and girls. They went from courtyard to courtyard, receiving nothing in return for their efforts. The Jews in the ghetto knew that the Germans had forbidden such things, for the Germans had not only taken away the lives of the Jews in the ghetto, but had also taken away the right to bury their dead with dignity. In the ghetto, the Germans had desecrated even death. At first the Jews were afraid to give up their dead, but finally that peculiar old man from the cemetery overcame their objections. Uncle Kiel and Mindel washed the dead secretly, dressed them in whatever they could lay their hands on, and said appropriate prayers over them. They worked from the crack of dawn till the stars made their appearance in the sparse ghetto sky, and though Uncle Kiel had never done such work before, he began to think of his labor as the Lord's work. His forty years working in the cemetery had not brought him so close to death as did working among the living Jews in the ghetto. He discovered that the slow agonizing process of dying is more horrible than the dead body itself. The first step in the torturous process of Jewish dying is the infiltration of the body by the plague ravaging the ghetto. The live Jewish body descending gradually to its death is blacker and deeper than death itself. Watching the death throes of the Jewish body, Uncle Kiel felt the Creator's angry hand and his great wrath. These dead Jews were not like the dead of days gone by. This death was a different kind of death, something more than death, a death that was not quite human, a remote and secret death that came from deep waters and boggy abysses, from a distant inhuman world. And the living intimate relatives who had turned over the naked body of the corpse also had some kind of distant, green glow in their eyes, the last human thoughts binding them to a strange and angry world.

At nightfall, Uncle Kiel and Mindel, both completely exhausted, finally returned to the little apartment. Mindel decided to cook some watery soup with gray greenish nettled leaves. After supper, Uncle Kiel couldn't fall asleep. For some reason, sleep had left him, and his eyelids, brimming with a gummy fluid, kept sticking together. He spent hours standing next to the wall, listening to the wind blowing into an empty sky. The ghetto wind always bears a sighing lamentation at night, like the sobbing of dying children. Several times he lifted his forehead and leaned it on the dark coolness of the windowpane, watching the pale passing cloud gliding like a dark ship over the rooftops. By that time, Mindel had long been asleep on the bench, every now and then mumbling something in her dreams. She dreamed of herself supporting and embracing the yellow emaciated bodies, washing them, and dressing them in old torn clothes and shirts. It was not until very deep into the night that Uncle Kiel lay down on the floor, put his prayer-shawl bag under his head for a pillow, and covered himself with some worn-out garment. In the small black window frame a green point of light shimmered through the night. That green twinkling star must have been the eternally watchful eye of God peering into the little room. That point was ever so distant, yet seemed to Uncle Kiel to be right outside the windowpane. Its beams of white magical light invaded the room and dazzled his eyes.

One night Uncle Kiel had a long and wondrous dream. Perhaps it wasn't a dream at all but a vision, because that green twinkling star kept shining throughout the episode. Arrayed before him in a circle were tens of Jews, young and old, with faint smiles on sad wrinkled faces twisted into unearthly expressions and grimaces. All were dressed in white robes with long baggy sleeves down to the lifeless hands that stuck out from under the white cloth. Their feet were hidden by the long gowns, which made it seem, as they approached, that they were floating on the grass. They encircled him on all sides, and in an instant, their faces were illuminated with a light that flooded every corner of the room. The light of the evening star outside the hut poured lavishly through every window and crack in the walls. All at once the heads and faces bowed to him and tried to grab his hands. He evidently heard them imploring him: "Rebbe, Rebbe—purify us!" In his dream he felt no fear—on the contrary, he tried to get to his feet and let them grab him by the elbows. He felt as if he were weightless as they grabbed him under the arms. Surrounded by this multitude of white-robed Jews, he led the way, while the walls of the room dissipated like morning mist. They went out into the courtyard, where it was still pitch black, and that enormous evening star guided them to the cemetery. The trees, bedecked in blossoms, came out to meet them with a song. And that song—a weird mixture of rustling leaves and falling rain— did not diminish but increased in volume as they drew closer to the burial field. Apparently, he had heard that song swelling from the death mounds before. It poured from the graves like a hidden river whose silvery waves constantly reflected the light from that one and only star in the green night sky.

Very early the morning after that strange dream, Uncle Kiel rose from his corner of the room restless and depressed. His beard rose and fell on his palpitating heart. He could barely get to his feet and walk to the window. Uncanny noises were coming from under the roofs. They had started some time in the middle of the night. The Germans had hurried the last Jews out of the ghetto. In the silence of the night the clouds sent from turbulent eastern waters brought with them distant echoes as well. They dispersed over the little streets like a melodious redemptive rain.

When Uncle Kiel and Mindele went through the gate, as they were accustomed to do every day, to start their rounds of secretly washing the ghetto dead, the wagoners were already driving their wagons filled with everything but the kitchen sink. A short distance away, some Germans were supervising the general confusion in the marketplace while others were chasing down Jews in the courtyards, rummaging through newly discovered hiding places, wells, and attics, and herding the captured Jews onto empty wagons. The Jews standing in the wagons looked up into the blank blue sky. Their eyes looked like extinguished flames or dried-up pools. As Uncle Kiel and Mindele emerged from the gate a tall German bolted out of a narrow alley and confronted them. In a panic, Mindel grabbed Uncle Kiel's coat as if trying to shelter herself under a large black wing. Uncle Kiel himself just raised his head a little higher than usual and looked straight into the German's face.

For a long time they stared at each other, locked together like two hostile animals in an unexpected encounter in the primeval forest. The mild-eyed Jew, with his disheveled red beard, thick bushy eyebrows, hairy neck and ears, gray-streaked side-curls, faced the transparently white, slimy, fishlike German who towered over the Jew like a huge wooden cross. The German wore a gleaming white shirt, and a pair of brown gloves covered his long thin delicate hands. They faced each other like day and night, two creatures from alien planets who had accidentally bumped into each other on earth. The Jew noticed that the German's eyes were a watery blue, like tallow, and his cheeks a fishy blue with thin veinlets close to the skin surface. A fiery spark was kindled in the eyes of the two adversaries, and both shivered. They stared at each other in silence. The encounter lasted no more than a moment but to both of them it seemed an eternity. The arrogant German's fishy eyes squinted mockingly as he felt his power over the nearby Jew who was no more to him than a twitching worm. The Jew, however, withstood the German's withering stare, blinking his bushy-browed eyes only for a split second. He stooped in front of the erect German with Jewish servility, but his subservient silence stemmed from the faith, passed down through generations, that God would triumph. The glances that crossed and locked together fleetingly constituted the clash of two powerful gods. While the German looked down at the Jew, certain of his superiority to the wildly overgrown creature who would soon be lying in pain at his feet, the Jew had raised his forehead and opened his bushy-browed eyes wider. The German now saw in those eyes a dark abyss spewing hellish flames. What followed happened so quickly that the German didn't even have a chance to move: the Jew clamped his black old grave digger hands like a steel hoop around the quivering fishlike throat of the German.

Overcome with fear, Mindel let out a wild demonic scream. Uncle Kiel and the German both fell to the ground in a heap, one

on top of the other, while the Jew's black hands refused to let up
their grip on the soft slimy throat of the German. The German
gasped for air as his hands twitched. The men grunted as their
bodies rolled on the ground. The Jew felt strength he didn't know
he had surging into his hands and forcing them deeper into the
German's throat. One moment the German was flailing in the air
and the next his thin outstretched body was lying under the grave
digger's naked chest. The brief struggle started so suddenly that
the Germans standing nearby did not move into action until both
bodies were lying intertwined on the ground. Uncle Kiel felt a
burning sensation in his shoulder, as if he had been stuck with a
hot needle. He heard the echo of a distant burst of thunder. Very
slowly Uncle Kiel's fingers loosened their grip on the German's
throat.

The German sprang to his feet. The other Germans laughed
while Uncle Kiel remained lying on the ground. Soon he also got
to his feet and walked shakily to the wagon, enveloped in total
silence. Mindel ran over to him and held him up as he walked. He
felt a soft warmth in his shoulder, as if someone were standing
next to him breathing on it. The Jews on the wagon stretched out
their hands and helped him climb aboard. Uncle Kiel and Mindel
were now crushed among the Jews, who kept whispering to each
other. She wiped the thick dark blood pouring out of Uncle
Kiel's shoulder as he leaned his limp body against the Jews trying
to support him. He felt his strength ebbing and his end approaching, and as he stood there his lips started mumbling something
inaudible. He silently thanked the Creator for having placed him
among so many Jews. But soon he started feeling bitter about
being forced to die an inhuman meaningless death. He prayed
passionately that the Creator would, at this very last moment,
grant his body a death worthy of a human being on this earth,
just as he, the grave digger, had provided legitimate ritual burial
to so many Jewish bodies. He prayed that he might die while
there was still one Jew alive in the ghetto. The Jews around him
would not let him fall. They continued propping him up even as
the dark blood formed an ever-growing puddle under their shoes,
making the bottom of the wagon look as though someone had
painted it red.

This time the wagon full of Jews didn't go to the railroad tracks. Rather, it wound along narrow side streets till it reached the wide green road that led directly to the cemetery. The road was lined with chestnut trees casting a velvety shade along the way. As the wagon rolled along the shady road, blossoms from the trees rained down on the heads of the Jews. When the wagon got to the cemetery, Uncle Kiel got down from the wagon; he had no idea how. The Germans had isolated him from the rest of the group, having prepared a special, more painful death for him. Mindel helped him the entire way till he fell to the ground. He realized that his prayer had not been accepted. With bowed head he took one last look at Mindel. The last shred of sky was reflected in her eyes. He lay on one of the mounds while Mindel stayed with him, not removing her hand from his bloodied jacket. He lifted his head as the Germans formed a circle around him and Mindel. His eye took in the little grave sites around him, age-old graves where generations of pious Jews rested. The gravestones reflected the rays of the silvery sun. Jewish prayers mixed with screams filled the air. A sweet scent of plowed earth blew in from the surrounding fields. The aroma of red raspberries descended like a soft curtain on the Jews. God's mellow enchanted fruit was overripe and heavy, swollen with bloodlike juice.

Łódź Ghetto, 1943

❖

The Wedding Coach

Dawn always occurred the same way. Someone would fling open a window and shout a wild, chilling death scream into the dark courtyard. At first the scream would cut the silence like a rusty knife; for a while it would hang over the sleeping courtyard. Then silence again. Ghetto windows reflected the brassy light of dawn. Outside the ghetto there must have been a real sunrise, but here only the heatless glow of distant fire.

Every day you could see solitary souls and still-intact families, rucksacks on their shoulders, kitchen utensils and other domestic implements in their hands. The women carried washboards, pots, and little tea kettles, while the old men clutched their precious prayer shawls and a hidden prayer book or Book of Psalms. Every now and then a woman would come to a complete stop in the middle of the courtyard, remind herself of something, and run back to her one-room apartment with a shout:

"Damn my soul, I forgot the tea strainer, people. . . ."

The people shuffling across the courtyard knew they were being stared at by neighbors who had not left yet. They sat half-naked at their windows, eyes bulging out of puffy faces, as they watched the rows of fellow Jews loaded down with belongings streaming out of the courtyard. The rucksacks were stitched together out of sheets and tablecloths, quilts and quilt covers, with Jewish names inscribed on them or embroidered on with thick black thread. They walked slowly, leading by the hand children who also had rucksacks with little plates attached to them hanging from their shoulders. Swaying under their heavy burdens, wiping the sweat from their faces, the deportees returned the stares from the windows as they walked on. They did not know where they were headed, but they were leaving the ghetto

with the vague thought that they would all meet again somewhere, those leaving as well as those left behind. Eventually they
would all be reunited, one by one—neighbors, relatives, all the
chosen people.

For the families in the apartments served with the yellow
paper announcing that everyone in the house was being deported
from the ghetto, life changed completely and instantaneously.
They immediately started hacking their wooden furniture into
kindling wood. Neighbors came to their aid and in return helped
themselves to various domestic items, utensils, and clothing that
wouldn't fit into the rucksacks. Strangers from the side streets
would hang around in the apartment rummaging through the
household goods. Nobody even noticed them. Neighbors
searched through the closets and ransacked the the drawers, taking a leftover plate or pot and sometimes a Yiddish book. Those
who had been ordered to leave, dazed and unstrung, circled
around the packed rucksacks at their feet. They had no way of
knowing what was happening to them. They couldn't figure out
why strangers from other courtyards were scavenging their
household goods. The closet doors hung open, and old clothes
were strewn all over the floor. Old landscape paintings and faded
family portraits hung on the walls, and long-dead family faces
gazed with congealed smiles at those who were preparing to go
on their journey.

When an apartment had been pretty much emptied out and
there was nothing more in the scattered refuse worth plundering,
those who had once lived there were finally left to themselves.
Alone in the dismantled apartment, they suddenly felt as if they
had somehow blundered into the purification shed where the dead
are prepared for burial. They bade farewell to the familiar faces of
uncles and aunts, casting a long last look at their matted beards
and Jewish wigs. For a long time they just stood in the corners of
the room as if to store up the domestic warmth for their sad journey. On the beds lay stacks of bedding that they couldn't fit into
their pack, no matter how they tried. The red bedding cast its
reflection on the wall like the glow of a raging fire.

When the people finally walked out of the apartment and left it
abandoned, they didn't bother closing the door. Neighbors stuck

their heads in but were afraid to go inside. As evening fell someone gathered a prayer quorum from the courtyards off the side streets and they started the evening prayers. A neighbor woman would tidy the place up a bit while the Jews prayed as fervently as if they were begging forgiveness for a corpse about to enter the world to come. The yellow patches on their shoulders flickered like the flame of a wax candle.

Fancy Jewish bedding was piled up to the rafters at old man Shmuel Dovid Pyetrikover's place. Before leaving the ghetto, evicted Jews would bring their bedding to old Shmuel Dovid and his wife. He had been worn down by years in the ghetto, and his wife never removed the old-fashioned wig from her head.

The deportees brought their pillows and mattress covers, tied up with bedsheets, to the elderly couple, who took in everything and threw it all onto a single pile that grew from day to day, until the bedding was piled up to the ceiling along one wall. People believed that the old couple would never be deported from the ghetto. They also believed that they themselves would soon return, reclaim the bedding, lay it out on their beds again, and rehang their kitchen utensils on the wall. For who knows what can happen? God might intervene—as they are heading for the train, their path may yet be blocked, and someone would say: "Where do you Jews think you're going? Get home. . . . You're no longer needed. . . . No more. . . No more ghetto . . ." And with their bags still packed, not missing a beat, they will stream back into the wide streets leading into the city, make their way back to the spacious apartments that had remained neglected all this time, head back to their stores and businesses, back to the study halls and synagogues, back to their lives as they used to be, as they used to be. . . .

But in the meantime the mountain of bedding at Shmuel Dovid Pyetrikover's kept on growing. The room was so cluttered that it was no longer possible to move around in it. Reb Shmuel himself lay under an enormous pile of bedding on an iron bed, and his wife's wigged head, withered like a dried fruit and bowed with years of famine and worry, was perched on her narrow shoulders like a sad, enchanted canary lost in the piles of bedding.

Reb Shmuel Dovid had not left his bed in months. His wife used to pour his excretions out the broken windowpane onto the little roof below, where a gathering of voracious crows cawed angrily.

Then a miracle happened. Everyone was ordered out of the courtyards and out of the dilapidated apartments, bag and baggage. But even this misfortune did not touch the Pyetrikovers. The neighborhood was completely deserted, but the two old people lay upstairs in their hovel, asleep and forgotten.

The weather turned cold and rainy. During the day the wind whistled through the broken windowpanes. But toward evening the skies would clear and become tranquil. A sea of flickering stars draped the windows like a green curtain embroidered with diamonds.

Reb Shmuel Dovid Pyetrikover had died painlessly, and his rigid body just lay there. Like most of those who died the ghetto death, he departed this life with a dream of peace in his watchful, watery eyes, which were still open. Not realizing he was dead, the old lady would get out of her own bed from time to time to adjust the pillows under Shmuel Dovid's head and feet, to make sure his body was shielded from the wind. She also crumbled some bread into a saucepan of water and set it at the side of Dovid's bed.

A small band of youngsters scavenged the abandoned apartments. They snatched up any leftover household goods that might be of value to the Germans. Behind them trailed a large wagon, which they loaded up with clothes and bedding. The wagon moved from courtyard to courtyard, from house to house, and eventually carried everything to the train depot behind the cemetery. On the evening of the day that Shmuel Dovid died, the wagon with the youngsters in it rolled up to the little house. They entered the hovel at the very moment the old woman had gone back to bed. A comforting dream had floated up before her aged eyes. Her deceased daughter, Ziesl, came into the room and asked her mother about her wedding. Ziesl still had the red fever spots that had covered her cheeks when she died of typhus in the first months of the ghetto's existence. With a smile on her face, Ziesl walked up to her father's bed, sat down on the edge, and ran her fingers through her father's beard. Later the old woman saw Ziesl standing next to her own bed, and felt Ziesl's burning hand on her shoulder.

She opened her eyes, and saw several youths bent over her in the darkness.

Rolling up their sleeves, they quickly grabbed her and lifted her out of bed. The old woman let them take her as if she were a helpless child, but she stammered:

"Jewish children, where are you taking me?"

"To a wedding, Granny . . . To a wedding . . . To a wedding in a coach . . ."

The children seemed to shimmer before her eyes, so the old woman shut them. Ziesl was sitting at her side again, and her face was flushed with joy as she spoke.

The youngsters carried the old woman through the corridor down to the wagon and set her down in it. Then they went back and fetched Shmuel Dovid. The youngsters grabbed him so that his lifeless arms curled around their necks. They brought him down as if carrying someone who had fainted, though his head, which had fallen backwards, rocked from right to left as if his throat had been slit. They hurried to load him into the wagon and get him covered with the mounds of bedding. This wasn't the first time they had loaded a corpse into the wagon that transported people out of the ghetto.

It wasn't until they had propped Shmuel Dovid up against the side of the wagon that they started throwing the bedding out of the apartment. The wagon filled up with cushions and mattress covers, with head pillows and cotton quilts. The pile looked like a red mountain that had just erupted in the middle of the courtyard.

All the while the youngsters were busy with Shmuel Dovid, the old woman did not open her eyes. The warmth of the bedding drew her into a deeper sleep. A gossamer strand of a smile settled like a sweet mist on her aged face. The words about a wedding that the youngsters had uttered as they were lifting her out of bed still echoed in her ears. Her daughter, Ziesl, with the red spots on her white face, was standing next to her again. Both of them rocked together leaning on the bedding as if they were seated in a luxuriously padded rich man's wedding coach.

The wagon carrying the two old people under the mountain of bedding slowly rolled out of the courtyard and through the black, empty streets of death, which were now cloaked in darkness. The sky once more bedecked itself with twinkling stars. As the wagon left the streets and entered the cemetery, a half moon mounted the night sky. The old woman lay in the wagon facing the sky, and Shmuel Dovid lay next to her, his lifeless eyes still open. The moon kept them company the entire journey. The sky, delicately shaded with stardust, kissed their white faces. The wagon raced across the soft, black earth, and the faster it went, the faster the moon pursued the two faces enveloped in the piles of bedding. Now the youngsters were urging the horses to a frenzied gallop. It seemed as if the wagon transporting the old couple out of the ghetto was about to leave the darkness of the ghetto behind for the open spaces of the star-filled night.

Łódź Ghetto, 1944

❖

Blossoms

Surveying what was left of the courtyard from the roof of the small wooden shack, Mendele saw only scattered piles of stones, the chimney of a wrecked building, and assorted bricks from other courtyards. Beyond the leveled courtyard, he could see nothing but ruins. The fences and walls that once separated one courtyard from another had been leveled, and what used to be a network of distinct courtyards was now one vast empty space. Of late, after his mother left for work, Mendele would rummage through the shallow gutters cluttered with shards of glass and old ironware.

From his vantage point on the roof, the scattered piles of stones and old utensils seemed strange and unfamiliar. In his disorientation, he turned in a circle, looking past the wire to the territory on the other side of the fence. He stared across the fence, wondering why he had known nothing about this place. He stood on his toes, shading his eyes from the sun with the flat of his hand, to get a good look. He stared till his eyes burned and filled with tears. He was still staring at the place where Jews no longer lived, when he heard a shout, and a shrill sound, like a whistle.

"Aii-aii . . . J-E-W-B-O-Y . . . J-E-W-B-O-Y . . . Aii . . ."

Mendele looked around but saw no one.

He couldn't figure out where the voice came from. There wasn't a living soul to be seen. Outside the ghetto, everyone was at work. In the unfamiliar non-Jewish courtyard across the way he could see a sparse little garden where a few small trees had just started blossoming. Two saplings were fully clothed in snowy blossoms. Several days ago, in that land where no Jews lived, the little trees had started blooming, and all the branches were blanketed in a mantle of white. The cherry trees had begun to blossom. Mendele's thirsty eyes couldn't get enough—in his entire life he had not seen so lovely a garden. Wherever he looked, there was white and green, green and white. The tranquil ground was covered with newly sprouted blades of grass, the trees were silver-white, spotted with bright red, as if on fire.

Mendele sensed he had seen something like this before, but couldn't remember when and where. It must have been a long time ago, before the war, and before the ghetto. It must have been in Uncle Michael's orchard before the Germans had taken his father away.

"Oh, my father, my father. . . . They took him away early in the morning, while he was at prayer, wrapped in his prayer shawl and *tefillin*."

Now, Mendele recalled that there had been trees like these in Uncle Michael's orchard, but with much taller, thicker trunks. There were apple trees and plum trees and a big tree with small green pears; there were even gooseberries growing on thorny bushes. What had there not been in Uncle Michael's orchard?

In the ghetto courtyards there were no trees. True, there was a wizened little excuse for a tree next to one of the shacks, but it wasn't in bloom; it looked like a broomstick pointed toward heaven. Last winter all the trees in the ghetto had been cut down, and for a long time had remained lying in the street, like dead bodies. His mother had said that the wood from the trees was for cooking, not for heat. One of those downed trees lay not far from their door, and it had even started sprouting little green leaves. In the Jewish courtyard there wasn't much green, but on the other side of the fence the whole world was in bloom, a joyous festival of leaves and blossoms. Though the garden on the other side of the fence was small, it was an unbroken sea of green. Grass covered the earth, and the trees were decked out as if for a wedding. The sweet fragrance of the grass hung in the air, spreading a mysterious tremulous enchantment. Again, Mendele heard a voice calling to him from the other side:

"Aii-Aii . . . J-E-W-B-O-Y!"

Mendele peered into the distance but still saw no one. Not a living soul was to be seen in the ghetto courtyard. Mother and the two young men who lived in the courtyard—keeping themselves alive by pulling the garbage wagon—were all at work. The voice could only have been coming from the other side of the little fence, where the trees were.

Who could be calling him? The voice must be coming from some hiding place. Suddenly, Mendele spotted a face peering out of a branch completely covered with blossoms. Its mouth was open, and its outstretched tongue was pointing at Mendele: "J-E-W-B-O-Y ... J-E-W-B-O-Y ... J-E-W-B-O-Y ..."

That there were no Jews living across the way, that there were people living there who didn't wear yellow patches on their clothing—of these things Mendele had long been aware. On several occasions his mother let slip that gentiles lived there, in a world not fenced in with wire. There, everything was permitted; you could walk on any street you desired. At times Mendele could hear the sound of an accordion coming from an open window, the sounds of laughter, and a sweet harmonica. At night, when Mendele was lying in the corner on the sacks of straw, unable to fall asleep because he was too hungry, Mendele often thought he heard silent echoes of mute melodies, as if a violin were weeping in the night.

Sometimes, pigeons from the other side, green-white and black-velvet doves, would fly across the fence and perch on the little roof. The other day one of them almost flew into their room. On another occasion a cat crawled across the fence onto the roof and spent the next few days next to the chimney. The cat had raised a racket, crying through the night for several nights, like a whining child; Mendele's mother swore her bitterest curses at the creature for keeping her awake after an exhausting day of brute labor. But Mendele befriended the cat. During the day he would stand under the roof and throw a little spool of thread up to the cat. Once, his mother had rushed out of their room, and screeched in an outlandish voice:

"You little brat, you murderer.... You've nothing better to do than play with gentile cats!"

Mendele, however, considered the creature less a cat than the wandering soul of a Jew who had sinned egregiously in this world.

All this flashed through Mendele's mind as he looked across the way, watching the face in the blossoming tree, with its tongue still pointed at him. He took a piece of broken mirror out of his pocket and caught the sun's rays, casting little sun birds to the other side. He enjoyed launching these sun birds over the dilapidated vacant ghetto windows. A silver streak of light bounced off the broken mirror in Mendele's hand and landed on the face in the tree. The face on the other side blinked. Blinded by the reflected rays of the sun, a child scampered down the tree and stood barefoot on the ground. He ran up to the little fence, clambered up a plank, and in no time the two children were face to face: Mendele on the little roof, the boy on the fence that separated them. The wire fence and narrow street kept them apart. From his perch, Mendele could see the black-and-red hut of the German guard at the other end of the street.

The children sat face to face, looking each other over in silence. For the first time they saw each other up close. Neither said a word. Mendele was scared his mother might show up right in the middle of things and reward him with a few whacks. But he so dearly wanted to have a branch with blossoms on it, just a tiny branch. He would plant it in the courtyard near their little chamber, and by late spring, the time of the Festival of the First Fruits, it would probably have sprouted another little branch. But how could he say what he wanted in gentile language? Mendele started gesticulating with his hands, pointing toward the trees in the strange garden across the way.

"Do you want?" the other called to him from across the way, pointing to the blossoming trees.

"Yes, yes, I want a branch, a green one . . . ," said Mendele, motioning with his head. "A small one, a tiny one, a tiny little one."

The other boy jumped from the fence in a single leap and ran toward the trees. Mendele's heart started pounding rapidly and fluttered anxiously.

"Please," he thought, "don't let anything unexpected happen!" As he watched, he saw the boy reach the tree and pull down a long white branch.

All of a sudden, someone grabbed Mendele from behind. It happened so suddenly he couldn't even catch his breath.

His mother was standing there, tearing her hair.

"Gev-a-a-a-a-a-l-l-l-l-d! Off the roof! You're going to bring a catastrophe on all the Jews, you rascal. . . ."

At this point, Mendele wasn't able to figure out a way to crawl down the roof without being grabbed by his mother, who would probably murder him.

He let himself down slowly, one foot at a time, and in springing to the ground ripped his sleeve. His mother grabbed him and started pinching his emaciated cheeks:

"You should only not grow up, thief that you are! Not enough that I'm a grieving widow . . . I have to feed a thief yet, a killer. . . ."

She dragged him into the room. For a long time, Mendele's sighs could be heard through the little gray window.

That night Mendele couldn't sleep. His mother's blows still smarted all over his face and body. When he finally did fall asleep, he dreamt a pleasant dream: he and his mother were strolling in Uncle Michael's orchard. It was late summer and the trees were heavy with seasonal fruit. Large plums on sagging branches, each plum as big as a fist, glistened with dew. Apples and pears lay scattered in the high grass. Uncle Michael, a tall man in a long black coat, told him to climb a tree and pick some cherries. After a tough struggle, Mendele managed to scratch his way up the tree. He straddled a branch loaded with blood-red and yellow-white cherries, then began to pick them, tossing them down into a straw basket. He picked some for himself and popped them into his mouth. They were tart-sweet and the juice overflowed onto his lips. He was bent over, straddling the branches of the cherry tree, so that he could barely be seen. His mother looked up at him with a smile. Uncle Michael was standing next to her. Down below they were busy emptying the little baskets which filled up very quickly. Mendele had stripped almost half the tree. He turned and tried crossing to another branch, when he unexpectedly saw a second boy sitting on a branch not far from him, also picking cherries.

He couldn't recall where he had seen the boy's face before, but he knew he had seen those eyes somewhere. The boy leaned over toward him and whispered in a low voice, so that Uncle Michael and his mother, who were below, should not hear:

"Do you waaaaaaaannnnnt? . . ."

"I want, I want," Mendele answered tremulously. The branch couldn't support his weight, and he felt as if it were going to break any moment and he would fall all the way to the ground. And now he actually felt himself falling, completely entangled in cherries, leaves, and branches. He was sinking into the depths, as if into an empty, bottomless well.

When Mendele opened his eyes it was still dismally dark in the room. A meager pinch of light from a sad sun filtered through a slit. In the ghetto the sun was always sad. His mother was standing over the spot where he was sleeping, shouting without pause:

"It probably has something to do with unclean cats and gentile boys. Is it any wonder that he rages in his sleep? . . . May all evil and bewitched dreams be visited on the heads of our enemies, O, Master of the Universe. . . ."

Mendele couldn't force himself to open his eyes. He imagined that Uncle Michael's orchard was still in full blossom. He couldn't understand why his mother was carrying on in this way so early in the morning. The light in the room quickly grew brighter, and particles of sun scattered through the room like a flock of summer birds. Mendele still couldn't bring himself to open his eyes. A cool breeze hovered over his face like a sweet dawn mist slowly rising from a meadow in blossom.

Łódź Ghetto, 1944

❖

Jewish Lives

RUTH LIEPMAN
Maybe Luck Isn't Just Chance

ARNOŠT LUSTIG
Children of the Holocaust
The Unloved (From the Diary of Perla S.)

ARMIN SCHMID AND RENATE SCHMID
Lost in a Labyrinth of Red Tape

WIKTORIA ŚLIWOWSKA
The Last Eyewitnesses: Children of the Holocaust Speak

ISAIAH SPIEGEL
Ghetto Kingdom: Tales of the Łódź Ghetto

ARNON TAMIR
A Journey Back: Injustice and Restitution

JIŘI
Life with a Star
Mendelssohn Is on the Roof

BOGDAN WOJDOWSKI
Bread for the Departed